YORKSHIRE'S
OLYMPIC
HEROES

HOW THE WHITE ROSE ATHLETES LIT UP LONDON 2012

NICK WESTBY

GREAT NORTHERN

Supported by:

YORKSHIRE POST

ACKNOWLEDGEMENTS

Although I was an eye-witness to the medals won by the county's athletes at the London 2012 Olympics, and have relied on my notes, recollections and the articles I wrote for the *Yorkshire Post* at the time, I am indebted to a number of secondary sources. National newspapers, regional newspapers and news websites were a constant source of extra material.

Thanks to the athletes for making the book possible with their sterling performances. I have been fortunate to speak with each of them either before, during or after the Games, and they are all inspirations in their own way. Following their journeys from Beijing to London and then on to the podium was a great thrill.

Thanks to Katherine Copeland, Tom Ransley and Nicola Wilson for their time after the Games, in filling in any blank spots in my knowledge.

Thanks to the *Yorkshire Post* for the access to the photographic archive and to the members of the sports desk for shaping me into a half-decent spinner of yarns. Thanks also to the Press Association for the pictures from the Games.

Barry Cox at Great Northern Books gave me the opportunity to put a memorable chapter of my own life into print, and for that I will be forever grateful. Thanks also to the team at Great Northern; Liz Slack, Patricia Lennon and designer David Burrill.

Editor Richard Coomber gave the manuscript a good old read, and also offered me a few tips along the way that proved invaluable.

A quick nod in the direction of the chaps I shared many an hour with in the regional pool at London 2012, who were amused and envious in equal measure at all the good news stories I got to write.

Great Northern Books

PO Box 213, Ilkley, LS29 9WS

www.greatnorthernbooks.co.uk

Thanks to a couple of *Yorkshire Post* colleagues. Richard Sutcliffe was a reliable sounding board, while Phil Harrison took the time to run his eye over parts of the manuscript. His pointers and advice were greatly received and appreciated.

Matt Westby proved an invaluable sub-editor of my first draft. He has an even broader knowledge of sport than I do and his fact-checking and eye for detail were of enormous help. The time he donated to the project will not be forgotten.

Finally, to my wife Amy, who had the original idea for this book. She deserves a medal for being a constant source of support and encouragement throughout the whole project. Her ideas were enthusiastic and enlightening, and like all the people who had a look at the chapters, her subbing was objective, clinical and of great help.

ISBN: 978-0-9572951-4-8

Edited by Richard Coomber

Photography: Press Association and Yorkshire Post Newspapers

Design and layout: David Burrill

Printed in Great Britain

CIP Data

A catalogue for this book is available from the British Library

CONTENTS

Supported by:

YORKSHIRE POST

INTRODUCTION

It was in the bowels of the Olympic Stadium towards the end of the second week of London 2012 when an unassuming scribe from a national newspaper tapped me on the shoulder. "Excuse me, are you the guy from the *Yorkshire Post?*" he enquired.

"Yes, I am," I snapped. "And no, I have no idea why Yorkshire athletes are doing so well. We like a shift at the coal face. We're not afraid to work hard. It's something in the water. Use any of those quotes you like."

It had been a long day, at the end of a draining, yet enriching two weeks. In following the exploits of the county's Olympians at the greatest show on earth, I had inadvertently morphed into the region's spokesman on why Yorkshire athletes had been doing so well.

I had expected to be writing stories of golden glory about Jessica Ennis, the Brownlee brothers, Andrew Triggs Hodge and Ed Clancy. They all delivered, emphatically so. But there were further stories of medal success in the shape of Nicola Adams, Katherine Copeland, Lizzie Armitstead, Tom Ransley and Nicola Wilson. Luke Campbell was also guaranteed a medal in the boxing ring by this stage.

It was a momentous Games for the county's representatives, who made their home towns and cities proud. Post boxes were painted gold in honour of our champions who came from the west in Leeds to the east in Hull, the north in Middlesbrough to the south in Sheffield.

By the start of the second week, the number of people who were suggesting, with tongue firmly in cheek, that if Yorkshire had been a country it would have been seventh, ninth, or how ever high on the medals table, was a story that began to take hold. National newspapers got in touch. "Why is it do you think?" they asked. The global news agency Reuters wanted to get to the bottom of the success of Yorkshire's athletes. I even appeared on Radio 4's Today programme to trumpet the success, even though investment in sport and the size of the county were thrown back at me as possible explanations.

But I or anyone else with the White Rose close to their hearts was not standing on a soap box proclaiming Yorkshire to be the sporting capital of the world. We were just immensely proud of our athletes, and rightly so, because like many of the home Olympians, they dug deeper than ever before to find the mental and physical strength to triumph on the biggest stage of all. There just happened to be a lot of them from Yorkshire.

As Olympics correspondent for the county's newspaper, the man lucky enough to be on the ground reporting from all these awe-inspiring sporting events, it was my job to convey how well each of our county's representatives was doing. In total, out of the 541 home athletes, 54 were either from Yorkshire, raised there, lived in the great county or had club affiliations.

Of the 65 medals Team GB won, 12 were forged in Yorkshire. Seven Olympic champions were crowned, two silvers were won and three bronze. Indeed, had Yorkshire been a country, it would have finished 12th in the table, just behind Australia but above the likes of the Netherlands, Spain, Brazil, South Africa and Canada.

Of the six gold medals won by British athletes on an unforgettable "Super Saturday", three of them were won by people representing Yorkshire. Either through individual brilliance or by being a vital cog in a ruthlessly efficient machine, that trio of athletes provided a snapshot of what would become a constant theme of that glorious summer. Hence the national interest in what was one of the novelty stories of an uplifting London 2012.

And the reason why that unsuspecting chap from a national newspaper had had the temerity to ask me if I was covering the Games for the Yorkshire Post. After I had spat out what

had become stock answers in a combustible fit of frustration and fatigue, the culprit In question rocked back on his heels, shrugged and said: "Well I was only going to say I know a couple of people you work with and they said to say 'hi'."

How embarrassing. Sporting heroes, whose every word journalists hang off, invariably manage to produce answers with good grace and humility. I had lasted barely eight questions before blowing my top. But no matter how tired I felt in that instant, and how grovelling my apology, I had been re-energised by the success of our Olympic heroes.

From Ennis, Adams, Clancy and the Brownlee brothers to Campbell and Armitstead, Yorkshire's stars rose on a wave of public euphoria to produce performances that will ensure they are remembered for years to come. And it wasn't just the Olympians that excelled. The Paralympic Games showed what disabled people can do, not what they can't do and produced more Yorkshire heroes to fete. Halifax's wheelchair sprinter Hannah Cockroft lit up the Olympic Stadium, while Lothersdale archer Danielle Brown continued her all-conquering sweep of major awards.

Why did athletes from Yorkshire do so well? There were several reasons. Investment, first and foremost, paid off. In the 1980s, Richard Caborn and Sheffield City Council invested millions into staging the World Student Games of 1991. The Attercliffe area of the city was regenerated as the Don Valley Stadium was built with the Sheffield Arena next door. They have been supplemented by the state-of-the-art facility that houses the English Institute of Sport. It is there, and next door at Don Valley, where Ennis trains. The EIS, as it is known, is also the base for Adams, Campbell and the British boxing squad, the men and women's volleyball teams and the country's disabled table tennis programme.

Ponds Forge International swimming pool was also opened before the 1991 World Student Games, a world class facility matched by the John Charles Aquatics Centre in Leeds, which is home to the successful City of Leeds Diving Club that sent five of its members to London.

The major universities of the county all embrace the importance of sport, particularly Leeds Metropolitan University, which attracts budding sporting stars from across the land to use its high-standard facilities.

The landscape of Yorkshire is also a contributing factor. The county is blessed with glorious if sometimes rugged countryside. The Brownlee brothers are often seen running around their home in rural West Yorkshire and beyond, while Armitstead honed her speed and stamina on the roads around Otley.

There is no disputing that this is a talented generation, thanks in some part to the investment in facilities. Yet without hard work, talent can lay dormant and unfulfilled. For me, the key ingredient and common theme among all the stories in this book is hard work and dedication. Each and every one of Yorkshire's Olympic heroes put in as many, if not more, hours than any of the opponents they faced at London 2012.

"Yorkshire athletes are not afraid to put a shift in at the coal face", was a phrase I used regularly during the Olympics. It was a colloquial line, one given with a pinch of salt and a tacit nod to the industrial heritage of the county. That hard-working mentality was best summed up by Jonny Brownlee, the 22-year-old who left everything of himself out on the triathlon course to win Olympic bronze.

"Two winters ago it snowed really badly in Yorkshire," said Jonny, whose brother Alistair won gold. "It was about minus 15 and I was mountain biking. Without realising I went across a lake. I slipped and my hand went through the ice as I fell. Half my body was frozen by the ice and I had to ride home for two hours like that, in the pouring rain. It's not always fun training in Yorkshire – but it makes you strong."

Indeed it does. And these Olympians made us proud. This book is a celebration of Yorkshire's Olympic heroes, how they became icons, what set them apart from the rest and what made them champions. It is about how they accomplished their dreams and wrote their own small chapter in the rich history of the Olympic Games.

Nick Westby
October 2012

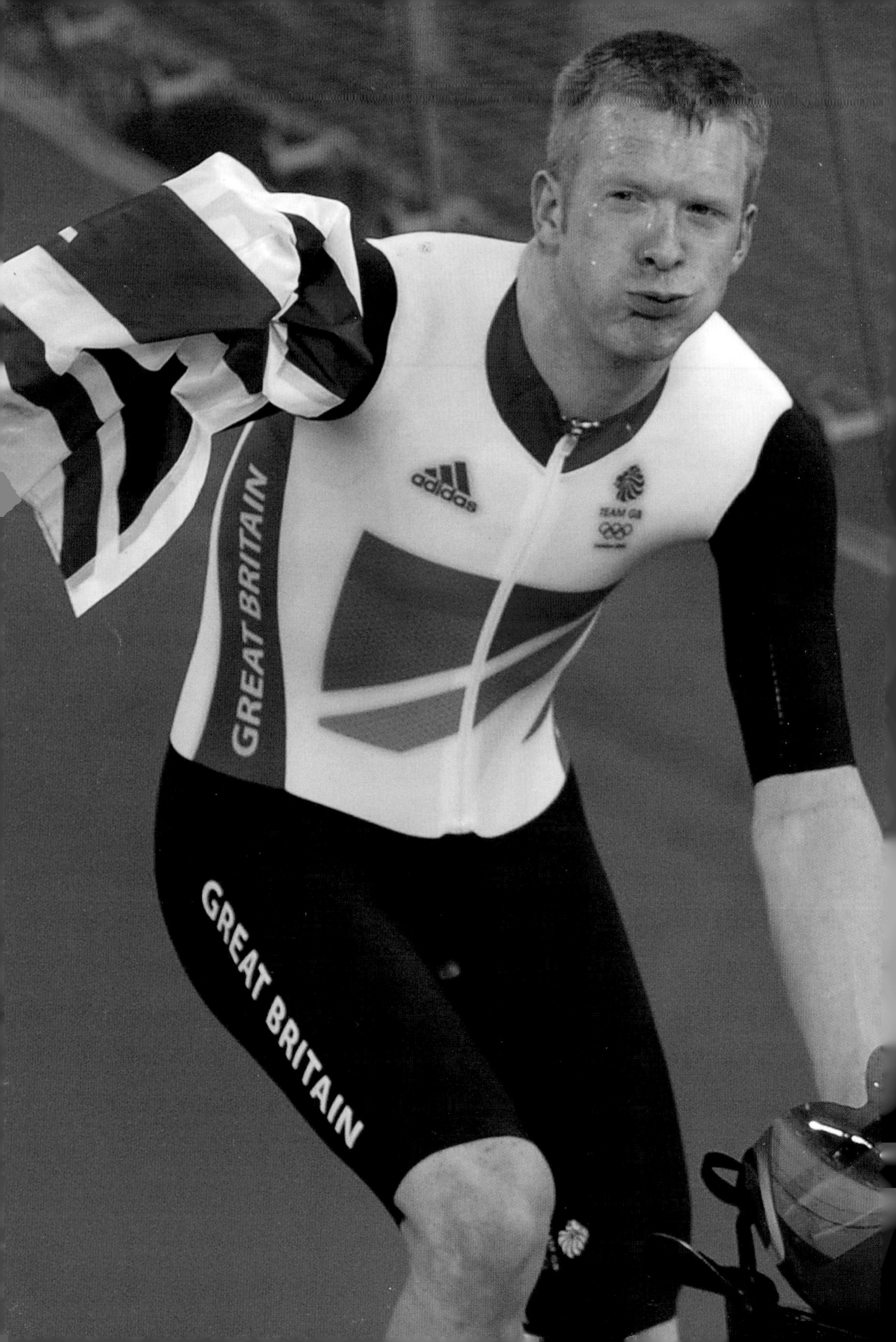
GREAT BRITAIN
adidas
TEAM GB
GREAT BRITAIN

1. ED CLANCY

Ed Clancy speaks like a young boy receiving his first bike on Christmas Day, not the natural born winner he is, when he says that his inner desire comes purely from a sheer love for riding a bicycle. It is that innocent motivation that provides the root of the success of Yorkshire's most decorated Olympian of the early part of the 21st century.

But he is a great deal more than just an enthusiastic cyclist. For Clancy, who was born on March 12, 1985, in Barnsley but raised in Huddersfield from an early age, is one of the best team pursuit riders in the world. And as he showed at London 2012, he is equally adept in multi-discipline events. A more laid back Olympic champion you could not wish to find. He has the unruffled air of Usain Bolt in the way he greets challenges with a shrug of the shoulders and a quiet resolve not to be beaten.

Yet there lies within Clancy an internal desire to be the best he can be - a trait that all great Olympians require. That he is able to satisfy that hunger owes much to his dedication and his tireless work ethic, which derives from his love for cycling.

He is blessed to work and train among the best track cyclists on the planet at the British Cycling hub in Manchester. There he feeds off great minds like Dave Brailsford and team pursuit coach Dan Hunt. He has prospered in the company of Sir Chris Hoy and Victoria Pendleton, the king and queen of the British track team who laid further claim to cycling immortality during the six days of track action at London 2012. That stable lived up to expectation by producing five multiple-medal winners in the tightly packed, atmospheric velodrome, including Clancy.

The Yorkshireman was already an Olympic champion, having struck gold in the team pursuit in Beijing in 2008. Alongside Geraint Thomas, Paul Manning and Bradley Wiggins who was contesting his third and final Olympics as a track cyclist, Clancy won the title in a world-record time against the quartet from Denmark. He arrived in London determined to defend the honour in an event in which he thrives.

Clancy was also scheduled to contest the multi-discipline omnium, an event making its debut in the Olympics after the International Cycling Union (UCI) moved to ensure equality between men's and women's track events after Beijing. The decision was controversial, with people inside British Cycling suspecting it had been done to weaken their chances of repeating the seven gold medals they won from 10 Olympic events in the Laoshan Velodrome in Beijing. What had been seven men's events and three women's, became an even split of five and five at London 2012, with the six-event omnium created to make-up for the reduction in individual events on the men's side.

Clancy –who burst onto the British scene in 2004 when he won the national madison title with future world road race champion Mark Cavendish - won the world title in the omnium in 2010 in Ballerup, Denmark. It was a result that took him by surprise, but together with that and a European title in the Netherlands the following year, he had done enough to qualify himself as Britain's representative in the Olympics.

Yet the schedule did not appear to work in his favour, with the opening omnium race, the flying lap, set for a 10.25am start just 16 hours after he hoped to be riding for gold in the team pursuit final.

A busy schedule was never something that

unduly concerned him. If anything, he was pleased to have the options. If he did both it would mean a gruelling nine races over four consecutive days. Whatever he decided, the team pursuit was sacrosanct. Clancy lives for the event. Riding together with his three team-mates provides him with a greater thrill than any individual accolades could ever generate. "I would trade a bit of glory for a win with the boys," was how he put it to the Yorkshire Post.

He convinced himself and the British team selectors that such an intense schedule was within the realms of his ability at the European Championships in Apeldoorn, in September, 2011. Clancy, along with Pete Kennaugh, Steven Burke and Andy Tennant, won the team pursuit title by five seconds on the Friday, before Clancy took omnium gold over Saturday and Sunday, the crown clinched in dramatic fashion as the Yorkshireman won the closing one-kilometre time trial and then was declared overall champion ahead of Frenchman Bryan

Coquard on a countback.

The performance of the British team in the Netherlands proved a watershed. In total they won seven titles from the 10 events that would be contested at London 2012. It came on the back of what had been a trio of performances in the world championships that fell below the very high standards the British team had set themselves in Beijing.

Just seven months after the unparalleled high of those Olympics, Britain were out of the medals in the team pursuit at the 2009 world championships in Poland, and languished third in the medals table overall. They were second in the medals table in Denmark the following year, with the team pursuit squad also beaten in the final.

And at the worlds twelve months later, again in Apeldoorn, Britain once more finished second in the overall medal count, with Clancy unable to defend the world omnium title due to illness. He was also nowhere near full fitness as Britain finished third in the team pursuit.

In each instance, Australia won the most medals, and in both 2010 and 2011 it was the quartet in gold lycra that won the team pursuit title.

The rise of the Australians and the lull in British performance resulted in a downgrading of expectations on the shoulders of the men and women of British Cycling leading up to their home Olympics.

Even at the World Cup meet in February, 2012, which doubled as the high-profile test event for the London Velodrome, Britain's team pursuiters were beaten by their Australian counterparts. The defeat served to spice up what was developing into an Ashes-style rivalry. With the world championships in Melbourne in April swiftly followed by Olympic competition in London four months later – the duel on the boards would be decided in the back yards of the two protagonists.

In any other year a world championship would be the pinnacle of a rider's ambition, but in Olympic year it represented only a stepping stone to the big prize. That was very much the case for the British team pursuit squad of Clancy, Steven Burke, Pete Kennaugh, Geraint Thomas and Andy Tennant that headed Down Under.

They went there determined to let the Australians know that even on their own boards, they would have a fight on their hands. The British quartet qualified for the final with the third quickest time in history. The Australians, not far behind, set the fifth quickest time.

It was game on and the final was a cracker. Britain had promoted Burke in place of Tennant and, after a terrific start in which the Australian quartet edged in front, the home riders of Glenn O'Shea, Jack Bobridge, Rohan Dennis and Michael Hepburn – roared on by their passionate supporters – would not relent.

Bobridge's Australian quartet had the slenderest of leads at 2,000 metres, the halfway stage of the race. But in a nip and tuck affair in which no quarter was given, Clancy's British team leapt out in front in the next 1,000 metres and opened up what appeared an unassailable lead of 0.8 seconds.

Back came Australia, with Clancy admitting afterwards that in those last few laps he was struggling to stay on the back wheel of the penultimate bike, and lead the charge when his turn on the front came. But they prevailed, just, ducking for the line in a world record time of three minutes 53.295 seconds. Australia were little more than a tenth of a second behind.

"That's the best race I've had," was Clancy's response at the time. "It's the ones that you really have to fight for that you remember and we won't forget that one."

Great Britain's performance director Dave Brailsford added: "That team pursuit final was the best race I've ever seen, not technically, but without doubt the closest and most enthralling."

The British team had made a significant statement of intent on foreign soil. They would

go back to training in Manchester and finalise preparations for the biggest test of the summer and of their lives, buoyed by their timely tonic. But they knew they couldn't rest on their laurels. If anything the Australians would come back even more determined.

Similarly, no success would come for Clancy if he were to wind himself up too tightly in the face of increased expectation. There appeared no danger of that In an interview he gave to the Yorkshire Post 100 days from the start of London 2012, when he alluded to his past accomplishments, Olympic, world and European titles and suggested that he was already content with his lot, that anything more would be mere icing on the cake.

"It is after all," he began, "just riding a bike around on a wooden board."

Yet beneath the cool exterior beats the heart of a fierce competitor. Playing it down was Clancy's way of unburdening himself of the expectation. He may have attempted to make light of London 2012, but deep down Clancy had enough motivation to go to his home Olympics and win a second team pursuit gold.

Everything had been pointing towards a strong defence of that title until a week to go before their London 2012 competition, when Welshman Geraint Thomas, Clancy's close friend, was struggling with food poisoning. It was not a major illness, but it was enough to disrupt the squad's final training sessions, and was hardly ideal. Thomas's illness hung over the team in the final days before the qualifying race on Thursday, August 2. Were illness to deprive the British team of Thomas – a champion in Beijing four years ago and a very able domestique to Bradley Wiggins on the road – it would be akin to a football team losing their striker on the eve of a cup final.

The illness was kept under wraps by the British team, but any misgivings they may have had were soon wiped clean by the wall of noise that greeted British riders in the London Velodrome. It is hard to imagine how 6,000 people could possibly make such a cacophony of sound. When British riders were involved in races the

atmosphere was electric, and knowing that such a deafening roar was being generated to spur them on to greater achievements, merely raised the performance of the home riders that extra per cent. If Thomas was feeling any ill effects, he was not showing it as Great Britain lined up in the qualifying round.

The crowd's anticipation seemed to be fuelled by the heat inside the velodrome. No outside air is allowed into the arena because of the effect it can have on the competition - the hotter the arena, the faster the bikes go – so the standard temperature was a sticky 28 degrees centigrade. The intense heat had an instant effect, as a host of Olympic and world records were set on that opening day.

One of those was by the British team pursuit quartet. With Thomas fit and healthy and joining Clancy, Burke and Kennaugh – with Tennant the unfortunate reserve – the home team admirably showed little regard for the qualifying round being merely a first hurdle, by setting a frenetic pace.

Cheered raucously by the crowd, their noise echoing around the unvented chamber of the velodrome, they crossed the line to qualify first in a new world-best time of three minutes 52.499 seconds. They were almost three seconds ahead of the Australian quartet who must have wondered just what revenge-seeking monster they had created. But there was no time to lap up the acclaim of the crowd to any great extent on that first afternoon. A world record would count for nothing if they did not deliver 24 hours later.

The second and final day of team pursuit competition saw the eight teams who qualified from the 10 starters of the day before, race twice. The first round would see teams competing against one opponent on the track, but also against the clock to determine whether they would race later in the afternoon for gold, bronze, or the places outside the medals.

To ensure a place in the final, Britain needed to produce another sparkling ride, yet with the expectation justifiably high that they would be good enough to be in the top two for the final just 90 minutes later, there was no need to break much more than a sweat.

What they managed to accomplish in qualifying first with a relatively comfortable ride, was to break the spirit of their opponents. In clocking three minutes 52.743 seconds against the Danish quartet – just a quarter of a second outside the world-best mark they set the previous day – Clancy and the team showed they were in a determined mood and had energy left to burn.

Australia were again the only team to get close, and that was still two seconds shy, although Bobridge, the 2011 individual pursuit world champion, kept his turns at the front short to keep something back for the final, in which, as was eagerly-anticipated, they would go head-to-head against Great Britain.

In between the first round and the final, the crowd were whipped into a frenzy as Victoria Pendleton won her second-round race in the keirin, that unique free-for-all which sees six riders jockey for position behind a slow-moving moped for five-and-a-half laps, before springing into full speed and sprinting for the line with two-and-a-half laps remaining.

As a bouncing crowd, which included Tony Blair and Bradley Wiggins, attempted to settle, the buzz was apparent. Two gold medals were within touching distance for British cyclists over the next hour.

First up, after a warm-down in the centre of the auditorium, and a few tweaks to bikes and tactics in their team pens, the men of the team pursuit squad in their red, white and blue lycra suits, with the bright red cone helmets, made their way to the start gate. Clancy had what for him was the ultimate accolade in front of him – a second team pursuit gold. All he, Thomas, Burke and Kennaugh had to do was reach out and grab it with both hands.

The Australian quartet of O'Shea, Bobridge, Dennis and Hepburn could not be overlooked. They remained a formidable threat. They had been stung by the pace and aggression of the home riders in the previous rounds, but were not about to let them have it all their own way in the Olympic final. Australians never give up anything without a fight.

Great Britain would have to seize the lead early and jump on Australia from the outset, never allowing their rivals to wrestle the initiative from their grasp.

Clancy – renowned as one of the best gate-men in the world for the way in which he propels his team forward from the start line - sat forward on his bike on the inside of his three team-mates, closest to the lowest part of the sloping track. His eyes looked straight ahead through his darkened visor to the first corner and the most decisive four minutes of his life. He rocked between resting on his black handlebars which pointed the way, and sitting back and upright as if leaning against a lamppost. Sixteen laps of the 250-metre track awaited and Clancy just wanted it to begin.

The noise in the velodrome quietened to an expectant hush as the beeps counted down and the cyclists set off, Clancy springing from the red metal trap that encased his back wheel. The Yorkshireman took the British quartet off at a blistering pace and after just a lap they had established a lead of 0.5 seconds. By the first kilometre, the lead was 0.3 seconds, with both teams now having found their rhythm and in perfect sync as the lead man swung off the front and dropped to the back in a perfect sweeping arc.

After six laps, 1,500 metres, Australia – their white helmets resplendent against the wooden boards - had reduced the gap to 0.167 of a second as the two four-man giants of track cycling attacked and counter-attacked.

But they would not get so close again. Australia's threatened retaliation was quickly neutralised by the British quartet, who with Thomas at the front of the train, re-established an advantage of half a second by the time the teams entered the second half of the race.

That third quarter was where Clancy and the team, cheered even louder every time they crossed the line, extended their lead by nearly a second to go into the final quarter 1.4 seconds ahead. By this stage the Australian train was down to three men as Glenn O'Shea tailed off, but still the British quartet – beckoned by the historic prospect of Olympic gold in world-record time – would not let their relentless pace ease.

Further and further they stretched the advantage on the overwhelmed Australians, whose resolve had been obliterated by the remorseless Britons. The crowd reached deafening levels as they crossed the line as champions. The speed gun registered 62.16kmph and the clock read three minutes 51.549 seconds, a sensational new world record. Australia were three seconds behind.

Clancy, the former Shelley High School pupil in Huddersfield, went straight to his team-mates and put an arm around their shoulder as they gradually slowed down. Then the Yorkshireman reached into the crowd and pulled out a Union flag, which he draped around him as he continued his glorious lap of honour. This was what had driven Clancy on during all those hard mornings of training, the love of riding a bike, and doing so in front of this magnificent, grateful crowd at his home Olympics.

"In Beijing I thought 'you'll never top that', but this is different," said an elated Clancy, nearly an hour after his crowning glory, and following another crowd-rousing gold-medal performance from Pendleton in the keirin.

"There was a lot of pressure on us, not just because we're Team GB at a home Olympics but because we're defending champions and the public expects. It makes it more meaningful, more for the fact that we've lost a lot of bike races along the way.

"We always knew when the Aussies turned us over here (in February, 2012) we had more to come. British Cycling is all about the Olympics, the process, and we knew there would be ups and downs. It's not nice losing events, seeing the best in the world go past us.

"But we had more to come in terms of tapering down and freshening up. We saw London (February, 2012) pretty much as a training ride. We said that at the time but I guess not everybody believed us."

Alluding to Thomas's illness, which hampered their build-up, Clancy added: "Not many people know that Geraint had a good dose of food poisoning a week ago and if he was on his A-game we would have gone quicker. He's one of the best riders in the world."

So is Clancy, but he would never say that. He had little time to trumpet his accomplishments or celebrate a second Olympic title with his team-mates. With the omnium starting the following morning, Clancy only had time to eat and rest before he was back in the velodrome in intense Olympic competition again. He was modest enough to know he had strengths and weaknesses in the event. His strengths lay in the pursuit, the flying lap and 1km time trial. His weaknesses were in the three bunch races; the points race, the elimination and the scratch.

If he was to be competitive against the 17 other world class riders, then a strong showing in the flying lap - a 200m time trial after a flying start - was imperative, no matter how burnt out he felt.

Any fears that he would be drained or not have anything left in the tank were quickly allayed as Clancy, roared on by the morning crowd in the velodrome, won the flying lap in a time of 12.556 seconds, ahead of New Zealand's Shane Archbold and Australia's Glenn O'Shea, neither of whom could beat 13 seconds.

The flying lap had been the perfect way to start the omnium for Clancy. It was one of his strongest events, required only a few moments of full exertion and

led into a seven-hour break before the competition resumed in the late afternoon.

Neither the points race scheduled for 5pm or the elimination race at 6.25pm were races Clancy relished. The Yorkshireman is at his best racing against the clock, not having to pick his way through other competitors who are crowding him out and negating his speed.

The points race is a gruelling 30km event involving all 18 riders who can claim points for intermediate sprints and lapping the pack. Clancy won a sprint to the line to take five points on just one occasion. It came with 85 laps remaining, which further emphasised the endurance these riders required. As it developed, the points race began to take on elements of a road cycling battle, with groups of experienced riders ganging up on the weaker cyclists, like Clancy.

The race finished after 40 minutes with Germany's Roger Kluge victorious and Clancy finally showing signs of fatigue, down in 11th. There was no time to dwell, as 45 minutes later the third leg of the omnium got under way. The crowd, which for the first time in three days in the velodrome had been numbed by the tactical points race, were lifted once again by a team pursuit squad, this time the victorious British women's trio of Laura Trott, Dani King and Joanna Rowsell who won gold in thrilling style.

The elimination race in the omnium is a far greater spectacle for the fans than the points race. Of the 18 riders, the cyclist at the back at the end of every second lap is eliminated, creating not only tension at the front of the bunch, but also at the rear.

From 12 riders remaining onwards Clancy was playing with fire at the rear of the bunch, and getting his back wheel burnt regularly. But the Yorkshireman hung in there, gamely.

From eight men left Clancy had to draw on all of his reserves just to remain in the race, sprinting past the back-marker on three occasions before finally succumbing in fifth place.

Bryan Coquard of France won a race that captured the imagination of the crowd, with Clancy's last-ditch heroics leaving him handily placed in fourth overall after two of his weakest events. He would return to the velodrome the following morning, with yet more glory within his reach.

By its very definition, the 4km individual pursuit should be an event that plays right into the hands of Ed Clancy. Contested over the same distance as the team pursuit, in which he is a master, it is about pure speed and technique.

Perhaps the only surprise that first Sunday morning in August was that Clancy did not win the pursuit. But he did enough to come second in a time of four minutes 20.853 seconds, just 0.2 seconds behind Denmark's Lasse Norman Hansen.

Clancy was back up to second place overall, tied with Hansen on 19 points, and trailing Australian O'Shea who had 17. But fourth and fifth were not far behind and Clancy's position was perilous. He required just two more superhuman efforts at the end of four of the most exacting days he could have imagined to give himself a chance of a third Olympic medal.

The penultimate event of the omnium was the scratch race, another test of Clancy's nerve and tactics in a bunch environment.

Sixteen kilometres of pure racing began at 5pm and Clancy was soon cut adrift in the second bunch as the pace at the front heated up. Clancy eventually finished the 64-lap race in 10th, which with one event to go, saw him drop out of the medal positions into fifth.

His hopes of becoming a double medallist, and so cementing his status as one of his county's greatest Olympians, hung in the balance. Winning one medal at an Olympics is a marvellous accomplishment. The chance to win two, and join an elite club, does not come around all that often.

The saving grace was that the final event in the omnium was the 1km time trial, a race against the clock, which Clancy lives for. With just one other man on the track at the same time, it's just the rider against the boards, testing his speed and his technique.

Clancy had the opportunity to lay down a marker as he was out in the third-to-last pairing, opposite O'Shea, with the leading four riders still to go. New Zealand's Shane Archbold had set the fastest time of one minute 03.290 seconds but Clancy was targeting closer to one minute flat. As ever, he burst out of the gate, throwing his weight forward to propel him on to the boards. Within seconds the black wheels were spinning furiously as Clancy, his hands thrust forward on to his handlebars as his legs turned in a controlled fury, ate into the track.

He completed the first 250-metre lap in 18.9 seconds, building speed all the time, with the vastly overpowered O'Shea already out of the equation on the opposite side of the track. Clancy's midway split was 32.909 seconds and still he was getting faster, his face grimacing as he almost drove into the boards, the Union flags waving frantically visible only in the corner of his eye.

He hit the final split in 46.821 and just kept getting faster and faster. Clancy crossed the line in one minute 00.981 seconds to take the outright lead in the 1km time trial, the speed gun clocking him doing 53kmph as he crossed the line. It was a time that would have been good enough to win a world silver medal in the 1km individual time trial at the 2011 world championships. It was a phenomenal effort given everything that was at stake and all he had been through in the last four days.

For raw speed, there is no-one faster than Clancy. But all he could do now was sit back and watch as the final four competitors attempted to beat him. If they didn't, Clancy's win would be good enough for a medal.

Coquard and Kluge were three seconds adrift, and then Italian Elia Viviani and Denmark's Hansen both failed to deprive Clancy of a second win in the six omnium disciplines.

Hansen came closest, clocking one minute 02.314 seconds, which for the Dane, was all he needed to secure the Olympic title. Bryan Coquard of France had done enough in the earlier races to win silver. The bronze, though, was still unconfirmed.

When the result flashed up on the scoreboards at either end of the velodrome, the packed arena burst into celebration, greeting the bronze medal for Ed Clancy as passionately as they had any of the seven golds Britain won on the track.

Clancy, his shirt unzipped down to his waist, embraced his coaches and support staff, and saluted the crowd. In four days he had contested nine races over two events, and won five of them. He had claimed an Olympic gold medal in the team pursuit and a bronze in the omnium.

"I came here for team pursuit gold and, as I always do, put all my eggs into that basket. Mentally, it was hard getting up the next day to go into a full-blown omnium," reflected Clancy. "It's an emotional rollercoaster out there. One minute you're winning the next you're completely out of the race. That was the story over the last two days.

"In the points race the guys tore me apart but that elimination saved my race. In the scratch I was in it to win it but didn't have the legs. I had the form of my life in the one kilometre time trial, the flying lap and the individual pursuit. I beat them by a mile. At one point I was looking like getting the gold, but in the scratch, it just slipped away. I knew it was touch and go whether I got a medal, but I want to say thanks to the team and everyone involved."

Clancy had experienced a London 2012 to savour. It was a career high for a man at one with his bicycle. With two gold medals and a bronze from two Olympic Games he took his place in the record books as one of the White Rose county's most successful Olympians.

2. ANDREW TRIGGS HODGE

Among the great duels of London 2012 - Michael Phelps versus Ryan Lochte in the pool, Usain Bolt against Yohan Blake on the track - the battle between the Great Britain and Australian squads in rowing's blue riband men's four developed into one of the more memorable rivalries. It was a contest built on an intoxicating mix of grudging respect, unashamed needle and a heavy dose of sheer bloody-mindedness from all eight combatants. It unravelled 35 miles west of the pulsing heartbeat of the Olympics, in south Buckinghamshire, on the picturesque water of Eton Dorney.

For two World Cup regattas and during the qualifying races for the final, the British crew of Pete Reed, Tom James, Alex Gregory and Yorkshire's Andrew Triggs Hodge, traded wins and jibes with the Australian quartet of James Chapman, Joshua Dunkley-Smith, 37-year-old Drew Ginn and William Lockwood. It all ensured a breathless final at a windswept Dorney Lake on Saturday, August 4, fought out by two crews who would rather capsize their boat than give an inch to their rivals. Their commitment, fight and talent made it a final worthy of any stage. The journey to it was no less dramatic, and provided one of the most compelling narratives of the first week.

The rowing regatta provided a feast of medals for the host nation as Britain continued its proud tradition of being the dominant force on the water, with three breakthrough victories for the women's squads. At the team's heart, the flagship boat of the men's four, had the chance to continue a sequence of victories that dated back to the 2000 Olympics, and one of the greatest moments in British sporting history. That day 12 years earlier, Sir Steve Redgrave won his fifth and final gold medal in a beguiling, edge-of-the-seat final, when his

row into the history books was threatened all the way by an Italian crew hell bent on tearing up an emotional script.

At London, the responsibility for continuing the legacy of what Redgrave had begun and Matthew Pinsent and his team had continued in Athens, rested on the shoulders of four men who knew only too well what was at stake. Four years earlier in Beijing, three of the men who would line up in the competition's first heat had themselves penned their own chapter in Britain's rowing chronicles.

One of those magnificent oarsmen was Hodge, an erudite, thoughtful individual, who studied to become an environmental scientist but chose instead to invest every fibre of his being into becoming an Olympic champion. Hodge was born in Buckinghamshire on March 3, 1979, but moved with his family to Hebden, near Grassington, in North Yorkshire in 1980. There he grew up until he left for Staffordshire University at the age of 18.

He took up rowing at university, and honed his skills as part of the Oxford University Boat Club having continued his education at St Catherine's College. Hodge helped the 'dark blue' crew win the University Boat Race in 2005, by which time he had already won a bronze medal in the men's eight at the world championships two years earlier, and competed in an Olympics. In Athens, Hodge was a member of the men's eight that missed out on a place in the Olympic final, finishing ninth overall. That was a result that not only crushed Hodge, but filled him with the desire and determination never to feel so low again on the biggest stage.

He channelled that anger, frustration and drive into the next four-year cycle, taking his place in the re-formed men's four following the retirement of household names like Pinsent and James Cracknell. Hodge finally realised his true purpose and delivered on his Olympic ambition when together with Reed, James and Steve Williams he won a pulsating final against the Australians to clinch Olympic gold in Beijing.

The British crew had only had six weeks to prepare for that performance, but still emerged triumphant. Four years later, with Alex Gregory – a reserve that day in China – replacing the retired Williams, preparation time would again be at a premium. For despite their history in the men's four, Hodge and Reed had spent much of the years between Beijing and London competing in the men's pair – and getting beaten.

The New Zealand duo of Hamish Bond and Eric Murray linked up in the wake of Beijing and went undefeated for the next four summers, culminating in a comfortable victory at the London Games. During that time they inflicted 14 straight defeats on Hodge and Reed, a sequence that included three world championship finals in Poland, New Zealand and Slovenia. Like every member of the admirable British rowing squad, Hodge does not train morning, noon and night to come second. There was no pride to be gained in showing off three world championship silver medals.

It led to some dark days for such natural-born winners during those lean years. As Hodge and Reed got up on chill winter mornings to push themselves to exhaustion, they found it hard to shake off the nagging doubt at the back of their minds that they were up against an immovable object in the Kiwi pair.

Hodge is an athlete who analyses performances and training techniques to the point of obsession. He takes his time before making decisions and articulating thoughts. But the ghosts of the defeat he suffered in Athens and the subsequent years of torture at the hands of the Kiwis were stalking him ahead of London. By the winter of 2011-12, and with his 33rd birthday on the horizon, those fears

that the coming Games could well be his last, were hitting home.

Behind the scenes, thoughts between himself, Reed and Great Britain's revered head coach Jurgen Grobler had begun turning to how they might get the best out of two of their leading male oarsmen. Hodge and Reed are natural leaders, and if the host nation were to prosper, then they needed their standard-bearers to lead by example. Finishing second in the men's pair would not accomplish that.

In April, after the British trials in which Hodge and Reed demonstrated their immense power by winning the men's pair, Grobler made the decision to move them into the four, alongside James and Gregory. Hodge went to the all-important stroke of the boat, with Reed placed in the middle, the engine room. They would have a little more than three months, incorporating three World Cup regattas and a gruelling high-altitude training camp in the Austrian Alps, to prepare for the defence of their Olympic title.

Hodge confessed to a little regret that he was leaving the pair having never out-paced and outwitted the Kiwi duo, but the overriding emotion was one of pleasure. He was back where he belonged. There was no time for nagging doubts over unfinished business. With only three months to go, it was all about focussing on the job at hand.

And few people are as focused as the former Upper Wharfedale School pupil. Hodge has tremendous admiration for the ethics of Grobler, who is as harsh a taskmaster as an army training officer. But the German is also a supreme tactician who since 1992 has shaped the British squad into the most feared on the water. Hodge speaks of his coach with the utmost respect. And the admiration is mutual, given how greatly Hodge is revered for his work ethic, temperament and will to win by all around him.

Hodge's first test back in his favoured boat came in Belgrade in early May at the first World Cup regatta of the summer. They passed the test with flying colours, claiming victory after getting stronger as the three-day meet developed. Hodge, though, would not let anyone get too excited. "By no stretch of the imagination is that a done deal," he said, mindful that the absence of the Australian crew made that opening win, creditable though it was, a hollow one.

The Australian four – dubbed the "oarsome foursome" by Drew Ginn - arrived in Lucerne at the end of May ready to do battle with their rivals, but their presence merely served to bring the best out of Hodge and the British crew. In the qualifying race Britain set a world's best time of five minutes 37.86 seconds. The shots across the Australian bow kept on coming in the final, in the two squads' first meeting of the year. As expected, the two boats went out fast and matched each other stroke for stroke with the Australian quartet ahead at the 1,500m checkpoint of the 2,000m race. Hodge gave the command for more from his crew. The GB stroke-rate increased and they powered past the Aussies to take victory.

If Hodge, Reed, James and Gregory had laid down a marker in their toe-to-toe duel, it was quickly ripped away by the Australians three weeks later at the final World Cup regatta in Munich. By then the quartet had been confirmed for London 2012 after GB Rowing announced their biggest ever squad for a summer Games – 48. But they were rocked on their heels by successive defeats to the Australian crew just six weeks from the start of Olympic competition.

Australia won the semi-final and then the final, taking gold in Munich by three quarters of a boat length. Defeat for the British continued an unwanted tradition that had begun in 2000 and continued ahead of Athens and Beijing, in that the British men's four had lost the last race before the Olympics. But in each of those years they had won when it mattered, claiming gold just weeks later. The burning question was would they do so again in London.

Hodge and his crew had much to contemplate as they headed off to their training camp in Austria. There was a concern that they were losing out to the Australians in the middle portion of the race, but the former Hebden resident was not unduly worried.

I caught up with him in Loughborough, at the kitting out of the British Olympic team in their official clothing. For Hodge, this public relations exercise was nothing more than a waste of time that ate into his precious training schedule. What he did say, though, was that the Australians would be foolish to read too much into their victory in Germany.

"We tried a few things out, we learned a lot about racing them and about our own tactics," he said. "We tried something different between the semi and the final, which definitely showed us a different avenue to chase, so we're very excited about developing that."

That process would continue at their training base in Berkshire and in Austria. The fortnight in the Alps was very much a back-to-basics experience that Grobler insisted upon to push his athletes to the very edge of their pain threshold. Isolated from everyone and everything, it was a camp that separated the winners from the also-rans. "It's an all-out camp and it's one of my favourite places because there's no hiding place," said Hodge. "It's a working camp in every sense of the word. You put your body through hell. If you don't go hard enough you get a rollocking from Jurgen."

Hodge had put his life on hold in pursuit of a second Olympic title, even admitting at one stage that he had felt the need to apologise to his wife - the former Dutch rower Eeke Thomee – for making her second best in the first year of their marriage. She herself was a former world championship competitor, so had a fair idea of the mental and physical preparation that Hodge and his team-mates were putting themselves through.

The day of the opening heats of the competition eventually dawned. Like much of the Olympic summer, the sun rose behind puffy white clouds that refused to be burnt away. Rain began to fall as the spectators made the long walk from the car parks scattered among the leafy suburbs to the temporary stands flanking the water on which battle would commence. Thirteen boats would contest the three heats of the men's four and 11 of them knew they were playing for third place. The title was destined to be decided by the British and Australian crews, who had duked it out the previous two months, each having given the other a bloody nose.

It may have been a completely different Australian crew that took to the water at Eton Dorney from the vanquished 2008 Olympic finalists, but the wounds from that defeat still festered. Aussies never like getting beaten by the Poms.

Drew Ginn's crew were also motivated by the prospect of rewriting history, by taking the scalp of the dominant force on their own water. He had raised expectation amongst his own team, and set the blue touch paper on the simmering rivalry by using his final press conference to say that the Australian crew "scared the hell out" of their British counterparts. He also alluded to the Aussie crew's fast starts as an intimidation technique to draw out the British, who were known to be faster finishers.

Ginn, a three-time Olympic champion and a member of the last crew to have bested the British in the men's four when Australia won gold in Atlanta in 1996, had the chance to prove those words prophetic in the first heat. Australia went out to lay down a marker, which is exactly what they did. They won their race comfortably in a time of five minutes 47.06 seconds, a new Olympic record.

Two thousand metres back down the water, the British crew had paddled into position to make their response. The moment of reckoning would not be for another five days, but if Hodge, Reed, James and Gregory were not in sync, then they would have to reach the final the hard way, through the repechage. Hodge would never let such standards slip, and roared on by 25,000 people who waved their British flags frantically, the home crew controlled their heat and won it by two seconds from the

Romanians, who were followed home closely by the quartet of Belarus.

It is foolhardy to read too much into the times of rivals who have competed in separate heats, because the pace is often different from race to race. Plus with their heat won, Britain were not going to expand any undue energy in an attempt to break a world record time. But the fact they stopped the clock at five minutes 50.27 seconds, three seconds behind the Australians' time, suggested that there was a bit of work still to do.

It was advantage to the men in green and gold vests, and Ginn, who was fast becoming the pantomime villain, saw the opportunity to add a little needle when he said: "We are not playing games. Any time you take it to people, there is fear and anxiety involved."

Hodge met the sledging head on. "The Aussies are great characters, they're always going to bring something to an event," he said. "They are lively guys. They play their game like we play ours. It's good to hear they've got a lot of fight in them. That's just what we need in an Olympic Games. I'm always up for a fight; it's what I love most, getting into a boat and going up against the best. We know what we've got. We know what we can do. Now it's time to race. We know we're going to have a big race and we're preparing to fight every inch."

Three days later the two crews met in the first semi-final, their first eyeball-to-eyeball confrontation since the final in Munich seven weeks earlier. Lined up alongside each other, the pace was frantic and the noise of the crowd, even 1,500 metres further up the course, was building.

True to their word, the Australians set a blistering early pace and led by a length at the halfway mark. But the British crew, roared into the home quarter by a corridor of noise from both sides, dug deep, smoothed their rhythm and clawed back the deficit before pulling away from the Aussies with 300 metres to go. Hodge, with the Australians in the corner of his eye, stroked the British boat home in a time of five minutes 58.26 seconds, with Ginn's crew crossing the line nearly a second later.

The Australian bravado of three days earlier had been quietened by the British crew's actions. Nevertheless, Hodge's response to the victory was cautious. "What was most satisfying," he began, "was executing a nice semi-final, having a really nice rhythm." Hodge is a person who will react if provoked, but he will not do the prodding. There was too much at stake, too little between the two crews to let verbal sparring detract from the mission at hand.

Hodge had said earlier in the week that the next few days would be like the last of his life, and nothing but complete focus on winning gold would suffice. The Olympic final was the culmination of not only four years hard work, but it would also be the defining moment of his life. He was a man who went into everything he did, be it a school lesson at Burnsall Primary or Upper Wharfedale secondary, or a training session at Caversham in Berkshire, with 100 per cent commitment. He never left anything to chance, or left anything of himself out on the water.

The morning of Saturday, August 4, would be no exception. The British and Australian crews had matched each other blow for blow in heat and semi-final. Now the vital matter of the Olympic final was here. A gusting cross-wind swept across Eton Dorney, buffeting the six crews who assembled shortly before 11.30. Because of the ferocity of the wind, and how much it would affect the crews' stroke and tempo, Great Britain opted to race from lane six where they would be most protected. It was their honour as the fastest boat in the semi-final, while the Australians were to the right of Hodge, Reed, James and Gregory in lane four. Sandwiched in between was the relatively young crew of the United States of Scott Gault, Charlie Cole, Glenn Ochal and Henrik Rummel, who had won the second semi-final.

Ginn had likened the Australian style to that of a drag racer, bursting out of the blocks and then progressively gaining speed until the end. But they were not prepared for the explosion off the start line that the British crew made. The hosts set the tempo instantly. Their rhythm was harmonious, their speed rapid, their early stroke-rate more intense than that of the men in green and gold.

Hodge set the tone as the cameras honed in on a face that was a picture of intense focus. At 500 metres, Great Britain had established a lead of 0.3 seconds on their rivals. Australia responded, increasing their stroke rate, but Great Britain maintained their relentless pace. Their oars were cutting into water and lifting out in complete sync, their bodies moving in perfect unison. By the halfway mark the advantage was 0.6 seconds, and still there was the factor of a vociferous British crowd to pull them over the finish line were it needed.

Ginn's crew needed to find something quickly. They kicked with 900 metres to go but they were greeted only with an even stronger retaliation from the home crew. Hodge has likened the boat moving so perfectly as "singing underneath them", and that is exactly what Britain's foursome managed in the Olympic final.

They hit the right notes 800 metres from home when Hodge, noticing the Australian attack to his right, countered by ordering James, Reed and Gregory to step on it again. They responded to the tune of a consolidated 0.6-second lead with 500 metres to go. Britain kicked for home in the final quarter. Those reserves of strength, built up on cold winter days of training, had never been more apparent. Their determination not to be beaten drove them on.

The hard work and sacrifice of the last few years had paid off. Roared on by a boisterous crowd that had the rickety foundations of the temporary stands shaking, Hodge and his team-mates crossed the line to take Olympic gold in a time of six minutes 3.97 seconds. The tradition had been continued in stirring fashion. Where Redgrave and Pinsent once strode forward for their country, now Hodge and his crew followed. The legacy of Redgrave's historic hour 12 years ago had

been in safe hands after all.

The gallant Australian crew, who had given their all and played their part in a terrific contest that captured the attentions of sports fans not only at Eton Dorney, but across the land, crossed the line 1.22 seconds behind the British crew to take silver. They could have no regrets. They had put every last ounce of effort into keeping pace with the British crew but had simply been beaten by a stronger, better unit. The United States quartet came home a further two seconds behind to claim bronze.

As those two crews bowed their heads in their boat or rocked back and looked skywards, gasping for breath, behind them the celebrations had already begun on the victorious boat. Hodge, so often a man to keep his emotions in check, let the unbridled joy pour out of him. From his seat in the stern, he looked to the right towards the stand that was still bouncing, roaring and waving its approval at what had just unfolded. Hodge kissed his wedding ring and punched his clenched fists skywards, repeatedly thrusting his arms in sheer delight at what he and his crew had just accomplished.

When they had circled round to the pontoon, stopping every now and again to pat each other on the back or acknowledge the crowd, Hodge leapt out of the boat and embraced Redgrave. He wore a smile as wide as Dorney Lake as he roared: "Bringing that gold home for Yorkshire. I'm on top of the world. We've sacrificed a lot in our lives to pursue this. We've all done so much to achieve this and it's a huge honour to be Olympic champions and in front of our home crowd. I'm humbled by it all."

Hodge was unequivocal in praise of his team-mates and the performance they had delivered. "We've had to produce one of our finest races in a four-year period and we did it today," he said. "These guys provided an impeccable race, it was executed to perfection. If we were Picasso that would be our masterpiece. It was an absolutely phenomenal race and to be sitting as the stroke of that crew,

I'm blessed.

"We looked back at the previous races and took a lot of inspiration from Munich and we stepped on. In the final we managed to underpin that with some very effective brute force. It was the complete package. Rowing is an infinite balance between technique and power and we struck that balance today.

"This is a top quality crew and I don't think any of us took winning for granted. We really got our heads down and took the race on because we knew we had to. We fought hard for that and we're just so thankful to everyone who helped make that happen."

On the medal podium under the shadow of the steep bank of the temporary stand moments later, the British crew collected their medals, a second gold for Hodge, Reed and James, a first for Gregory, and then turned to their Australian rivals and pulled them alongside as the national anthems began to play. Like all great sporting enemies, they had forced each other to dig deeper than ever before, to call on reserves of strength and willpower they never thought they had within them in order to beat the other. But when the honours were decided there was nothing but respect between the two. The crews of Australia and Great Britain made London's men's four a terrific contest. They pushed each other so hard that it ensured only the maximum of effort would reap the ultimate reward.

The admiration between the two crews continued as they sat beside one another in the post-race press conference 90 minutes after their epic final. Hodge expanded on what he had said earlier about the tactics and the enormous power required, and how big a role the home crowd had played.

But he gave most away when it was Drew Ginn's turn to speak. The South Australian had been the chief architect of the banter of the past few days that at times echoed a boxer promoting a world title fight. But when asked if this first silver would spell the end of a hitherto gold-medal laden Olympic career, he showed his vulnerability and his humility as he choked back the tears.

"For me at 37 I would love to go on but it takes a lot," he said. "You just don't back off. You dig deep inside yourself. It takes a toll with family. I always said beforehand that I would take the time afterwards to assess the future but the reality is I have had two back surgeries. Just being here was something. After Beijing (when he sustained a back injury that gave him leg discomfort for a year) I was not sure I would row again. Quality of life was an issue."

Ginn could barely manage any more words as he was consoled by Joshua Dunkley-Smith to his left. Sitting another chair on, Hodge watched with a look of complete empathy across his face. Everything Ginn said struck a chord with the big man from North Yorkshire.

He knew better than anyone the questions Ginn was asking of himself, about how much time and energy is invested and how many personal sacrifices are made for what ultimately boils down to just a six-minute race.

At 33, Hodge was beginning to ask himself those same questions, just an hour and a half after the greatest moment of his sporting career. Ginn's tears and words hung in the air of a marquee that was thick with emotion. After the press conference had finished, and the medallists could at last begin to unwind by spending time with the families who had been both their support and the victim of their greatest sacrifice, Hodge moved straight for Ginn to give his great rival a hearty embrace and share a few words with his friend and foe.

Hodge's London 2012 journey was complete. It had been a massive, life-affirming success. Looking back on all the hard work, the hurt of defeat he had suffered in Athens and then again in the three years in which he and Reed toiled in the men's pair, there was only ever going to be one outcome for the Yorkshire-reared Olympian.

Those failures merely strengthened his resolve. They transformed him into one of the most driven Olympians not only on the rowing squad, but on the entire British team.

3. KATHERINE COPELAND

Twenty minutes after that unforgettable mental and physical battle in the men's four at Eton Dorney, one of the more surprising and uplifting tales of British success at London 2012 unfolded. As Andrew Triggs Hodge and his victorious crew celebrated euphorically a victory that was as expected as it was emphatically delivered, the six boats contesting the lightweight double sculls final made their way quietly to the start gate 2,000 metres away.

Among them in lane six was the surprise package of the home team. British women had already risen to the occasion earlier on in that first week, with Helen Glover and Heather Stanning, and then Katherine Grainger and Anna Watkins ensuring the host nation would at last have its first female Olympic rowing champions.

But there were no such expectations on the two women lining up for the lightweight double sculls final on Saturday, August 4.

Sophie Hosking, in the stroke seat, was the 26-year-old daughter of 1980 men's eight world champion oarsman, Peter Hosking. She had been part of the fabric of British rowing for nearly a decade without finding her true calling.

Sitting in the bow was the slender, unassuming figure of 21-year-old Katherine Copeland, who was born in Northumberland, before moving to Ingleby Barwick in Stockton-on-Tees near Middlesbrough. Kat, to her friends, had only been partnered with Hosking for four months. There was no back catalogue of heartache or triumph for these two. No rivalries developed, no expectations raised, no inspiration to be derived from previous torment.

At the start of the week Copeland and Hosking were considered outside medal chances at best, and what a seal that would put on a breakthrough Games for British women rowers.

It might have appeared that Copeland had nothing to lose, but there was a sense within this 59kg bundle of determination that this was an opportunity she might never get to grasp again. Even at 21 she had fallen in and out of love with rowing enough times to know deep down what the sport meant to her. That it already defined her.

What had often been a love-hate relationship began for Copeland in her schooldays. As she came to the end of primary school before heading to Yarm School, the 11-year-old was presented with a list of pursuits, ranging from beekeeping to photography to sport, that she could do in an activities week. Among them was rowing.

Her father Derek suggested she try rowing because at the time, the young Kat Copeland was chubby, and Derek thought that would translate to strength in the boat. But Copeland was racked with fear that she would struggle at sport, and self-conscious about her appearance. So she picked photography.

It was not until she was 14 that she finally took up rowing at the school which sits on the River Tees. Even then the decision was made more for social purposes than with any grand designs on one day becoming an Olympic champion. She started to row because her friends did.

To her surprise, Copeland was pretty good at it. Her coach at Yarm School, Andy Clark, saw potential within the first six months. "The attitude was always there," said Clark, in an interview with the Middlesbrough Evening Gazette. "She was always wanting to get out on the water and always asking questions. She was very frustrated if she didn't get things right. There was something about her."

By 2007 she had been brought to the attention of the junior British rowing selectors and made her first appearance at the Coup de la Jeunesse – an international meet for under 18s. At the two-day event in Italy, 16-year-old Copeland won gold in the women's quad. Twelve months later at Inniscarra Lake in Ireland, she won gold again at the Coup de la Jeunesse, this time in the single sculls.

By then she had already graduated to Tees Rowing Club, where she came under the umbrella of coach James Harris. Her progress continued to be rapid. At the Australian Youth Olympic Festival in 2009 she won a pair of medals, a gold in the quad and a bronze in the lightweight double. Then in July, Copeland - who was still only 18 - finished fourth in the single scull at the under-23 world championships in the Czech Republic.

The potential was obvious, but the next move would threaten to end her growing passion for the sport. Copeland convinced herself that if she wanted to become a better rower, she would have to move to London, where she would get greater exposure.

"When I left sixth form I didn't really know what I wanted to do," she said. "I thought I'd row full-time and see where that took me. A lot of rowing is based down south and I thought that if I want to be the best I've got to be down there. But I didn't think it through. I didn't like not having other things to occupy me when I wasn't rowing. And I didn't click with other members of the club I joined. I put up with it for a year but in truth knew I wasn't happy from minute one."

Copeland was homesick the entire time. It is a brave thing for a teenager to venture off alone, and equally courageous to stick it out as long as she had when things clearly weren't working. She had grown up a lot and still finished sixth in the lightweight double sculls at the under-23 world championships in Belarus.

But the truth was Copeland was falling out of love with rowing. "I stayed for the year because I didn't want to be the person that quit," she said. "But because I wasn't happy, I wasn't rowing very well."

Something had to give, and in August, 2010, at the age of 19, Copeland moved back north and into her parents' home in Stokesley, North Yorkshire.

"The grass isn't always greener," she said. "When I got back to Tees Rowing Club I realised how good the river was, how good the club was, the coaching and the people. I appreciated it a lot more."

Back under the guidance of James Harris, back among friends and family, Copeland's passion for rowing was reignited. When she returned to London eight months later for the British trials, she did so a better rower and won the lightweight single sculls.

The summer of 2011 would prove a breakthrough as she won the under-23 world title in the single sculls, and a silver in her first senior World Cup regatta in Munich. She also finished fifth at the senior world championships in Slovenia, having won both the heat and the semi-final of the lightweight single sculls.

By the start of 2012, Copeland's stock was rising. She again won the British senior trials final in the single seater and was on course for London. "I only went to the trials to see if I could do it, because if I didn't I would have regretted it for ever," she said.

Having proved her capabilities, there was a potential snag. There was no lightweight single sculls discipline in the Olympic programme. The only boat she could go into was the lightweight double, and Hosking was already established in that alongside Hester Goodsell, the pair having won a bronze medal at the world championships the previous year.

But Copeland had overtaken Goodsell as the premier sculler and in April, Britain's Australian-born head coach to the lightweight and women's crews, Paul Thompson, put Copeland and Hosking together for the summer.

Even though their total time together in a boat was effectively only a week, Copeland was comfortable with the experienced Hosking, who she had roomed and rowed with on previous training camps. "We haven't got loads of time but I think we've got enough time," said Hosking.

Copeland was initially put into the stroke seat, with Hosking in the bow. The move yielded instant dividends. Copeland and Hosking won a silver in the opening World Cup regatta in Belgrade in May and then finished fifth in Lucerne later in the month.

After finishing fourth in the final regatta in Munich at the start of June, Thompson made the decision before taking his women's team to their pre-Games training camp in Italy, to switch Copeland to the bow seat, and Hosking to the stroke, in an effort to generate more power.

The switch was untested in competition by the time they sat at the start gate at Eton Dorney for the opening heat of the Olympic lightweight double sculls competition. Nerves were etched on the faces of Copeland and Hosking as they steadied their boat at the start.

They were in lane six, with the New Zealand pairing of Louise Ayling and Julia Edward – the fastest crew in the world so far that year – in lane one. The dangerous Danish pairing of Anna Lolk Thomsen and Juliane Rasmussen - who had beaten the British girls in the final regatta in Munich – were in four.

Trailing the Kiwis at 500 metres, the British pair stepped on the gas for the second quarter of the race and by half-distance had established a lead they would not relinquish.

Such was their composure, and their rhythm, that Copeland and Hosking stretched their advantage further over the closing stages with a dominant demonstration of sculling. They crossed the line so far ahead of the Danish crew that they looked like they were on the water for a casual Sunday morning row. The official time was six minutes 56.96 seconds, comfortably the fastest of the 17 boats that contested the three heats. From a crew that had shown little previous form, it was not only a significant marker, but an anxiety-free performance that belied the magnitude of the occasion.

Any hope among the anticipated medal-challengers from Denmark, New Zealand, Greece or China, that Copeland and Hosking were a flash in the pan, were blown out of the water in the semi-final four days later.

Even alongside the world champions from Greece, Christina Giazitzidou and Alexandra Tsiavou, with the German crew also fast, there would be no let up from this surprise package of the Olympic regatta. Even when they languished in fourth place at the 500-metre marker, their rivals seemingly reasserting their authority, they would not give in.

Copeland and Hosking trailed the United States, Germany and leaders Greece, but yet again they pulled it back in the middle portion of the race. Keeping their heads straight and their stroke-rate controlled and high, the home duo rowed through the US and German crews and pulled to within two tenths of a second of the Greek duo, who 1,000 metres earlier had held a 2.4-second advantage.

Roared on by a deafening crowd as they rowed passed the grandstands, Copeland and Hosking got stronger and stronger. In that last 500 metres they turned a 0.2-second deficit into an advantage of three seconds as they shattered any illusions that their performance in the heat had been a fluke. The Greek world champions simply had no answer as Copeland and Hosking underlined their growing status with a winning time of seven minutes 5.90 seconds.

Their performance in the semi-final not only made their rivals stand up and take note, but also Sir Steve Redgrave, who was working as an expert pundit for BBC television. The five-time Olympic champion said: "It was unbelievable, in the terms that Greece were dominating last year. Our girls stuck to their tactics, looked relaxed and cool and came through."

Two mornings later, at a blustery Eton Dorney, the day of reckoning dawned for Copeland and Hosking. The young North Yorkshire woman stared straight ahead as she waited for the Olympic final to begin. She was attempting to shut out the magnitude of the race that was about to unravel. She was trying to forget the anguish of her year of torment in London, and trying to remember all the good that had been taught to her by James Harris at Tees Rowing Club.

Nothing could be gained by looking towards the bike-mounted coaches to her right, who were gathered on the bank looking just as nervous as any of the 12 women who were attempting to row into the history books. Equally, only fear awaited her if she looked ahead to the finish line, which was flanked by 25,000 spectators packed into the grandstands surrounding the closing 250 metres, serving only as a distant reminder of the enormity of the occasion.

Copeland tried to imagine the Olympic final was a regular regatta. She had spent all week shutting the possibility of standing on the medal podium out of her mind, because the thought of it reduced her to tears. For the next seven minutes all she and Hosking had to do was focus on the task at hand, put everything they had worked on over the last four months into practice and execute their stroke to perfection.

If there had been a weakness in their opening two races, it was that they had started slowly before building to a victorious crescendo. In the biggest race of all they started quickly, putting in a fierce first 100 metres from lane six, which they had chosen as fastest qualifiers because it offered greater protection from the cross-wind.

The Greeks, though, would not be subdued so easily, and gathering speed every time their oars split the water, Christina Giazitzidou and Alexandra Tsiavou edged into the lead. They still led at 500 metres with the Chinese pairing of Dongxiang Xu and Wenyi Huang – sandwiched in between the two European

crews in lane five – second, ahead of the British boat.

But as they had all week, Copeland and Hosking found their rhythm in that second quarter of the race and began eating into the slender advantage of the crews ahead of them. By halfway they had rowed through the Chinese boat, their bowball scything through the water like the blade of a saw and inching ever closer on the Greeks in lane four.

With 500 metres left the British duo were a length ahead of the Chinese who had nosed in front of the slowing Greeks. Britain had assumed control of the Olympic final. All week they had got faster the further the race unfolded and so it proved again.

Copeland was a picture of calm. Her breathing was measured as she yelled "come on" to the back of Hosking's head in front of her, glancing casually to her right to see the sought-after image of the entire boat lengths of the chasing crews.

"I don't remember the middle of the race," recalled Copeland. "But with 750 metres to go I started thinking we could do this. Then as we got close to the line all I was thinking was 'just don't mess this up because you're not going to get this chance ever again'. I was just hoping we didn't catch a crab, where the blade goes into the water at a funny angle and affects your rhythm."

But it seemed that not even striking the back of a blue whale could have disrupted the harmony of the British scullers as they hit 38 strokes per minute and powered towards the finish line.

The crowd cheered deliriously, hardly believing what they were witnessing. British rowers were enjoying the regatta of their lives and this unheralded duo were thrusting themselves into the spotlight with every stroke.

Victory was never in doubt over those closing 500 metres. If anything, it was a full-speed lap of honour as the delirious home crowd greeted their achievement. Copeland and Hosking won gold in a time of seven minutes 9.30 seconds.

They became the first British Olympic champions in the discipline. Dongxiang Xu and Wenyi Huang of China were second, almost two seconds adrift, with the spent Christina Giazitzidou and Alexandra Tsiavou hanging on for bronze for Greece.

What happened next was one of the more moving images of not only the golden summer of 2012, but of a monumental 'Super Saturday' when Britain won six gold medals. Kat Copeland sat with her jaw dropped in disbelief and her eyes wide in amazement. The magnitude of the accomplishment was too much for her to comprehend. Hosking, in front of her, had already buried her face in her hands. As the 26-year-old from London Rowing Club eventually coaxed her aching limbs into movement and swivelled round to greet her friend, her partner and her fellow champion, Copeland was still struggling to process what had just happened.

They stared at each for a few seconds as the boat slowed of its own volition, the cheers of the crowd in the background still echoing around Eton Dorney. Then the enormity of it all sunk in so hard it took Copeland by surprise.

"Oh my God we won the Olympics!" she screamed as she embraced Hosking. "We're going to be on a stamp."

Of the myriad enduring images of a memorable London 2012, the disarming disbelief on the face of Copeland is one that will linger long in the memory. It was uplifting and emotional, and brought home to those watching just what the Olympics mean. Copeland was the Kat that got the cream.

Ten minutes later, after thanking her parents for helping her through the dark days live on national television, Copeland dropped to the floor exhausted. Fatigue and emotion had overcome her and it nearly made her sick as her legs turned to jelly and she grabbed for support and gasped for air, waiting for the calmness that she exuded at the start of the race just 10 minutes earlier to return.

"My mind was blank," she said a few weeks later, the size of the accomplishment even then still not fully appreciated. "I just couldn't believe what was happening. I was just shocked and really overwhelmed. I was just so happy, and couldn't believe it was happening.

"But you don't realise how tired you are. I finally realised after the first interview. I just started crying. I just couldn't believe it. Sophie had to do all the interviews, I just felt so sick and so tired. I was so overwhelmed. I just wanted to sit down."

Copeland's disbelief was not echoed by her mother and father, who had watched in awe and unparalleled pride as their daughter won Olympic gold.

Mum Penny said: "We are so proud of her. I keep telling people my daughter's in the Olympics. Now I can say she's got a gold medal." Dad Derek added with the confidence only a parent can impart in their child: "I always think Kat is going to win."

Mother and father watched with tears in their eyes as 45 minutes later Copeland and Hosking received their gold medals. The two champions were in fits of tears, giggles and smiles as they continued to wrestle with the emotion of the occasion and their accomplishment.

In their post-race press conference, Copeland said: "I wish we had known this would happen a couple of months ago when we were having such a stress. I wish I'd have known three years ago. We saw people win gold medals and I really didn't see myself as any of those people."

Katherine Copeland never believed she belonged in a British rowing squad that boasted the names of Steve Redgrave, Matthew Pinsent and Andrew Triggs Hodge – men she had watched and drawn inspiration from. After lighting up London 2012 with one of the most heartwarming stories and evocative images of that Olympic summer, she had better believe it.

4. JESSICA ENNIS

As the morning sunshine crept above the triangular floodlights atop the Olympic Stadium on Friday, August 3, the 80,000 people in the iconic venue rose as one to welcome their hero. Jessica Ennis strode into the stadium shortly after 9.30 on the first morning of track and field events. The 30th Summer Olympiad was already seven days old, but there was a palpable sense among all who were present in the Games' centrepiece stadium that it was about to come alive as the blue riband athletics events began.

There was no better way for the starting pistol to sound on nine days of athletics than with the opening act of the women's heptathlon, and the first chance for Sheffield's Ennis to live up to her billing as the Games' poster girl. All 38 heptathletes stood on the back straight facing the crowd as they were introduced, the loudest roar of all, almost loud enough to scare off the gathering clouds, reserved for Ennis. The 26-year-old took a step forward and waved to all corners. The moment she had been waiting for had arrived. No amount of expectation can prepare a home athlete for the wall of noise they are greeted with, and Ennis was visibly moved.

The relief when the formalities were over was there for all to see. Along with the women who were out to deny her what had been foreseen as her destiny, Ennis returned to the call room adjacent to the starting blocks on the home straight to wait for her turn to re-emerge into the Olympic cauldron for the 100m hurdles, the first discipline of the heptathlon. Ennis would go in the fifth of five heats, with her time to be measured against everyone.

The £1m track at the London Olympic Stadium was expected to create a host of world-record times during the 2012 Games. It featured technology that rebounded energy from the sideways movement of an athlete's foot. In those opening four heats, which featured two of Ennis's great rivals for the title, Ukraine's defending Olympic champion Nataliya Dobrynska and Russia's world champion Tatyana Chernova, no-one showed any signs of threatening world records. Indeed, no-one ran under 13 seconds.

What her rivals did, however, was of no concern to Ennis as she removed her training top and crouched into the blocks in lane eight. The stadium clock read 10.29. The starter prepared the field, the boisterous crowd gradually fell silent, and the gun went off, echoing through the eerie quiet before sparking an instant eruption of noise as the British fans roared their superstar on.

What followed in the next few seconds shaped the entire heptathlon competition. Ennis, having waited for this moment since she was 11 years old, exploded out of the blocks. Leading with her left leg and ensuring her stride pattern stayed consistent for the entire 100 metres, Ennis hit the front early and just got quicker and quicker as the race unfolded.

Sara Aerts of Belgium outside her and Jessica Zelinka of Canada pushed her as far as they could, but their pressure served only to make Ennis run even harder, much to the delight of the crowd whose noise was increasing in decibels with every hurdle overcome.

There was never any doubt she would win the race, but the manner in which she did sent shockwaves through the competition. Ennis's time of 12.54 seconds was the quickest ever by a heptathlete. It was the fastest ever by a British woman in the hurdles, and only 0.33 seconds slower than the world record set by Bulgaria's Yordanka Donkova in 1988, the year she won the Olympic final in Seoul.

What's more, it matched the time American Dawn Harper ran to win gold in Beijing four years earlier.

Needless to say it was a personal best for Ennis, and gave her the lead in the competition. She looked ecstatic and saluted the crowd for their role in inspiring her to the finish line, her smile lighting up the Olympic Stadium.

"I can't believe the time, I'm in shock," said Ennis immediately afterwards. "I felt ready for the event after all my hard work and training, but I didn't think I would do that great. I was nervous but strangely calm."

The blistering performance earned her 1,195 points, but more than that, it was a significant statement of intent, that on this, the biggest stage of her career, Ennis meant business. It was an ominous warning to the other competitors.

****

Jessica Ennis was ten years old when she went to Don Valley Stadium in Sheffield in the school summer holidays of 1996 to attend a Start:Track meet. The purpose of the event was to identify young athletic talent. Ennis, born to a Jamaican father Vinnie Ennis and British-born Alison Powell, had little background in athletics. Yet she won a pair of trainers in the competition.

But more importantly that afternoon she caught the eye of Sheffield athletics coach Toni Minichiello, who had seen enough raw talent and energy in the slight-looking young girl to work with.

What impressed Minichiello was the sheer speed of a junior who had received no prior training. What helped the process was that Ennis instantly fell in love with running. Within a year she had joined the City of Sheffield Athletics Club, where she officially came under the tutelage of Minichiello, who despite being impressed with her speed, felt that a young athlete of 11 should be taught all disciplines to help her develop into a stronger competitor.

Ennis, who attended Sharrow Primary School

and then King Ecgbert School in the affluent village of Dore, made her debut in the English Schools Championship two years later and by 2000 was national schools champion in the high jump after clearing a height of 1.70m. More national accolades followed, with her first major junior international events taking her to Canada in 2003 and Italy in 2004. She was developing into a multi-discipline athlete, with her speed turning most heads. But in her early days it was at the high jump at which she was most successful.

****

The bright blue summer sky had begun to darken as the second event of the women's Olympic heptathlon began. The high jump had been a speciality of Jessica Ennis in her early days, her personal best of 1.95m set in 2007 being the joint-best height recorded by a British jumper. But she had not beaten that mark for five years, making it the only event of the seven in which she had, literally, not raised the bar.

Held under the shadow of the Olympic torch in the eastern end of the stadium, Ennis declined to enter the high jump contest at the opening height of 1.71m, and as expected, had little trouble in clearing 1.74m and 1.77m at the first attempt.

Each jump she executed was greeted enthusiastically by the crowd, who already sensed in the wake of that phenomenal start in the hurdles earlier that morning that their golden girl was on a march to the top step of the podium. Ennis, though, knew she could not get ahead of herself, mindful of the ills that could still befall her in such a demanding sport.

Indeed, a first reminder of the fine margins of top level sport was only moments away, as on her first attempt at 1.80m Ennis clattered the bar and knocked it tumbling to the mattress. Involuntary gasps could be heard around the stadium. Retreating to her seat in the dugout as her competitors took their turn, a quick glance to Toni Minichiello in the stands helped keep her calm and unflustered.

Ennis nailed 1.80m at the second attempt and

to reassert her confidence, then required only one jump at 1.83m to move on to the next height. By now, with the rainclouds having emptied a brief deluge on the track, only the leading contenders remained, with American Hyleas Fountain - the Beijing silver medallist who was third after the first event – the biggest threat to Ennis.

But by failing with her first two attempts at 1.86m, Ennis cranked up the pressure on herself and once more raised the tension levels inside the Olympic Stadium. Again it was a quick look to Minichiello that helped sharpen her focus, and with shorter intervals between jumps with so few competitors left, Ennis sprang into action to the left of the high jump area.

The crowd, clapping in unison, watched as Ennis, arcing around smoothly, launched herself off her right foot and executed a near-perfect leap that saw her ease over the bar. As she landed she turned to a delighted crowd and bounced twice on the mattress, joyously clapping her hands as she smiled triumphantly.

It was another significant marker laid down under maximum pressure. That she failed to clear 1.89m on her three attempts did not matter too greatly. The fact that she had reached that level, with only four other competitors, meant her lead would be intact. Ennis finished fifth, collecting 1,054 points.

Fountain could not clear 1.89m, with victory in the high jump going to Lithuania's Austra Skujyte, the heptathlon silver medallist in Athens in 2004, who cleared 1.92m. But it was the girl from Sheffield who went into lunch on that first day the happiest.

****

Having competed to a high standard in international junior and student events the world over, a 20-year-old Jessica Ennis arrived in Melbourne in March, 2006, for the Commonwealth Games as understudy to British favourite Kelly Sotherton.

Sotherton, the bronze medallist from Athens two years earlier was favourite to land gold in Australia, and did so. But it was the performance of Ennis that made pundits sit up and take note, and also confirmed to the young Yorkshirewoman that she belonged on the biggest of stages. The girl from the Steel City had travelled to Melbourne with the expressed aim to set a new personal best, and score more than 6,000 points in her first senior major international meet. She did even better than that. In recording 6,269 points, Ennis improved her personal best by more than 350 points, with lifetime highs in the high jump, the 200m and the javelin.

It was enough to earn her a bronze medal and the first major international podium of her career. It was a significant achievement and one that illustrated that Ennis could thrive in the biggest competitions. Although she finished eighth at the European Championships later that year, in Stockholm, Ennis again set a new personal best score of 6,287, to further illustrate her growing status on the world stage.

****

For a woman as slight as Jessica Ennis, the shot put is never an easy pursuit. It is a discipline that is often the domain of athletes with tremendous upper body and leg strength, and something Ennis has had to work hard to stay competitive in.

Having rested during the afternoon, she returned to the stadium for the first evening session of athletics, in control of the heptathlon competition. What had been a breathtaking performance in the morning, though, would count for nothing if she did not build on it in the final two events of day one.

Winning the shot put outright was beyond her, especially after an opening throw of 13.85m, but with the sun ducking down out of view of the stadium, and the evening temperature dipping, Ennis came up with a throw on her second attempt that kept her in the hunt. As she waited her turn she prowled around the in-field with only her thoughts to occupy her, the tension building all the time. As she approached the throwing area she looked a picture of concentration. Ennis bent down, wheeled around and, pushing off with her legs, hurled the shot 14.28m.

It was the best she could manage in her three throws, but shy of her personal best. It was, though, very respectable, with the majority of her competitors all failing to break 15 metres. Only two managed it. Nataliya Dobrynska of the Ukraine was the defending champion who had ripped the world indoor pentathlon title from Ennis's grasp earlier that year. She recovered from an average morning with a throw of 15.03m. They were all behind Austra Skujyte, whose distance of 17.31m was a new heptathlon record. It was the Lithuanian's second win in three events and it moved her to the top of the standings. The eighth place Ennis achieved earned her only 813 points, which was good enough for second place overall.

****

Austria, May, 2008, and the picturesque town of Gotzis was the scene for the last heptathlon competition before the Beijing Olympics. Jessica Ennis, fresh from a fourth-place finish at the world championships in Osaka the previous year, was fine-tuning her preparation for her bid for glory on her Olympic debut later that summer.

The Hypo Meeting was a significant signpost on the road to Beijing. Who was in top form in Olympic year? How close to becoming a major force was 22-year-old British star Ennis? Sadly, the world would have to wait for those answers, for after the first day's competition, a pain in her right foot was sharp enough to force Ennis to withdraw from the competition.

Injuries are not something to trifle with in Olympic year, and every precaution was taken. But there were worried faces among Ennis, Toni Minichiello and the support staff. Those fears were confirmed a few days later when scans revealed Ennis had suffered a stress fracture in her right foot. It was a heartbreaking blow. Ennis was out of the Olympics. Her coronation as the new queen of British athletics was put on hold.

If an athlete is lucky they might get to compete in four Olympics. At the age of 22, injury had forced Ennis to wait another four years before she would get to compete on the greatest stage of all.

****

The shot put had not been perfect, but Jessica Ennis was still in control of her Olympic destiny at London 2012. Lithuania's Austra Skujyte was a field event specialist, and her rise to the top of the heptathlon standings after three events owed everything to her victories in the high jump and shot put.

Ennis was a stronger all-round competitor and there was no need for panic. There was no time, in fact, for the Yorkshire woman to be worrying about her position. The demanding test of seven events over two days is as much about mental strength as it is physical. Champions are not made from competitors whose emotions are all over the place. And what's more, the closing act of a pulsating opening day of the heptathlon – the 200m – was scheduled to start in a little over an hour.

As the competitors returned to an Olympic Stadium that was close to rocking, Ennis - as one of the fastest sprinters in the competition - again found herself in the closing heat of the event. From lane seven, with the camera flashes erupting like fireflies in the night sky behind her, Ennis sprang out of the blocks and gained quickly on the bend on the two women outside her, one of whom was her British team-mate Katarina Johnson-Thompson.

Ennis dragged Canada's Jessica Zelinka with her on her inside but the British sweetheart was a good ten paces behind Dafne Schippers of the Netherlands in lane one. Schippers was a 200m specialist who had run in the individual final in the European Championships earlier that summer and would later that week run for the Dutch 4x100m relay team in the Olympic final.

But Ennis, her desire overwhelming her fatigue after a draining first day, hunted the Dutch girl down over the closing 80 metres. Zelinka was left trailing in her wake as Ennis confronted a slight headwind and ate into Schippers' lead. As Schippers visibly tired over the closing ten metres, Ennis remained strong, refusing to accept defeat. The two ducked for the line at the same time, another two metres, and the victory would have clearly been Ennis's, rendering the referral to a photo finish irrelevant.

As it was Ennis and Schippers stopped the clock at exactly the same time, 22.83 seconds. It was a second personal best of the day for Ennis, and a second maximum-points return from four events. Her time equated to 1,096 points and ensured she ended the opening day of the competition with 4,158 points, the third highest first-day total in history.

More importantly, it was good enough for a lead of 184 points over Skujyte, with Zelinka in third. Her perceived big rivals for gold, Tatyana Chernova and Nataliya Dobrynska, languished in ninth and tenth respectively. There remained much work to be done on the second and decisive day, but there could be no disguising the fact that Ennis had taken a significant step towards the Olympic title on a blistering first day.

"I feel tired but I'm absolutely made up with the day," she said. "To perform like that with two personal bests and to end with a PB in the 200 is a brilliant start. Coming in I knew I was in good shape, but I could never imagine performing like this. I've definitely exceeded my expectations."

****

The British public love a fighter. They love a story of triumph over adversity. What Jessica Ennis accomplished in Berlin in the summer of 2009, only sealed her place in the nation's hearts. The despair of Gotzis just weeks before Beijing took a while to get over. Ennis found it difficult to watch an Olympics she knew deep down she could have thrived in.

Instead she turned her attentions to getting fully fit again and beginning the Olympic cycle to London in the best way possible. That would

mean winning a world title in Berlin, which she set about doing with her customary determination.

Her performance was the high point of the world championships from a British perspective. Ennis went in front from the first event and never relinquished the lead. It was a coming of age for the 23-year-old, who became the country's first heptathlon world champion.

She set a personal best in the shot put and a new career-high score of 6,731 points. After the pain of Gotzis, nobody who watched her triumph could not revel in her joy. The young woman from Sheffield had finally arrived as a global superstar.

****

If there were any question marks over Jessica Ennis's prospects of winning gold in the London 2012 Olympic heptathlon, it centred over her ability in the long jump and the javelin, the fifth and sixth events of the competition. Both field events had deprived her of major titles in the past, and the long jump in particular, had been a nagging concern for much of the build-up. In Istanbul just a few months earlier, she conceded her world indoor title to Nataliya Dobrynska with a poor long jump, and in the British trials in Birmingham in June she fouled three times.

Her personal best was 6.54m which she had at least threatened by jumping 6.51m in each of the last three seasons. They were not world-beating lengths, but if she could get near them in London, it would be a good result. The injury she suffered in Gotzis in 2008 had also had a knock-on effect, forcing her to switch her take-off foot from right to left.

When she returned to the Olympic Stadium on Saturday, August 4, for the biggest day of her career, she did so looking to build on her lead rather than protect it. Attack was the best form of defence, but when she only managed 5.95m with her first jump into the unbroken sand, Toni Minichiello in the stands felt his heart sink.

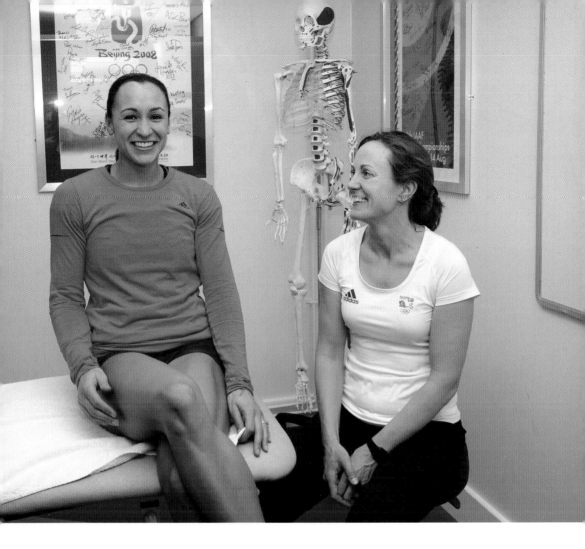

"That was the only time where she gave her old coach a few palpitations, that and for a little while in the high jump," said Minichiello, who like the rest of us, must have feared that the marvellous form of the previous day had not followed Ennis back to the track on the Saturday.

He and the British public need not have worried. Ennis, the courageous fighter she is, dug deep and executed two superb long jumps in the second and third rounds, getting better with each effort as she leapt 6.40m and then 6.48m.

Symbolically it was a big leap towards the Olympic title for Ennis. Any hope that her first jump had left the door slightly ajar for her rivals was shattered as Ennis slammed it shut again with those final two jumps. The only woman to jump further was Tatyana Chernova, who after a poor first day, had thrust herself back into medal contention. But the race for gold was gradually becoming a one-woman show.

Ennis stretched her lead from 184 points to 258 with just two events remaining. The grip was tightening.

****

Jessica Ennis arrived in Daegu, South Korea, in August, 2011, as the undisputed world No 1 multi-eventer. In Barcelona the previous year,

she had added the European heptathlon title to the global crown she won in Berlin, and was back to defend in the Far East. She also held the world indoor pentathlon title, won convincingly in the spring of 2010 in Doha.

Her path to London 2012 so far had been serene. However, in major competitions in the year leading up to the biggest competition of her life, Ennis would encounter a few bumps in the road.

In Daegu, Ennis lost her world title. She was beaten by Russia's Tatyana Chernova, despite outpointing her opponent in five of the seven disciplines. Her defeat highlighted the importance of every single event, and how mistakes or poor form in just one can be the difference between the major champions people remember and the second-place finishes people forget.

Ennis struggled in the javelin, managing 39.95m compared to the 52.95m Chernova threw. It equated to a points-swing of 251 and although she beat Chernova in the closing 800m, the damage had been done. "Javelin has been one of my weaker events, but I've never performed that poorly," she said at the time.

The wake-up calls kept coming. This time it was seven months later in Istanbul where Ennis lost her world indoor pentathlon crown. This time it was the long jump that proved her downfall, Ukraine's Dobrynska there to capitalise on the mistake to lift the title.

In hindsight, those two defeats served Ennis well. The pressure on her shoulders even months in advance of the Olympic Games had become almost unmanageable, and something none of the other British medal hopes ahead of London 2012 – with the exception of teenage diver Tom Daley - were experiencing.

The losses also allowed Toni Minichiello to work his pupil even harder on the events that were undermining her. They also further inspired the inseparable duo to give everything they had in Olympic year to help Ennis achieve her ambition to win gold. Just as the heartache of the summer of 2008 made them better, so would the pain of defeat in the world finals in Daegu and Istanbul.

****

There was no better place to exorcise the demons of Daegu than with a javelin in her hand in the penultimate event of the Olympic heptathlon in London's Olympic Stadium. Despite leaping toward gold with her courageous response in the long jump just 90 minutes earlier, the haunting memories of Daegu and how a lead could quickly evaporate were fresh in the morning air of London.

Weaker individuals might have succumbed to those soul-destroying negative thoughts, but not Ennis. With the Olympic title within touching distance, there was only going to be one outcome in the javelin. Any concerns that she might struggle were wiped away with her very first throw. Ennis, undaunted by the enormity of what was in front of her, ran in a controlled fashion to the line, keeping her body straight and her focus sharp and threw the javelin 46.61m, just half a metre shy of her personal best. The crowd roared their approval. Ennis turned on her heels, a beaming smile radiating from her face.

If there was any doubt, it was gone a few minutes later when with her third throw Ennis set a new personal best in the javelin of 47.49m.

It was again a controlled piece of execution and was good enough for 10th place and 812 points. Much more than that, though, it effectively sealed the gold medal for the Sheffield woman. She had cleansed the ills of Daegu and Istanbul in one morning's work, all with the bravery and sheer desire that marks her out as a champion.

****

Preparation for the London 2012 Olympics began for Jessica Ennis on an unseasonably warm South Yorkshire morning in October, 2011. Ten months of a six-day-a-week training regimen would follow as Toni Minichiello

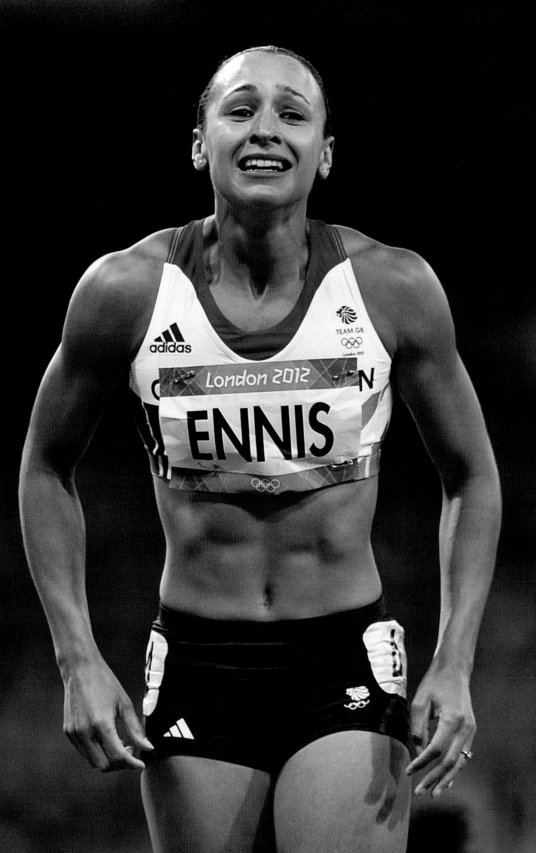

oversaw a demanding programme for his star pupil. With Ennis in her mid-20s, the time for major changes to schedules and techniques had passed. What Minichiello was trying to achieve was a fine-tuning of her performance that would lead to greater consistency.

All of which was done around Ennis's home in the leafy suburbs of Sheffield and at the English Institute of Sport in Attercliffe, a state-of-the-art facility that is just a javelin throw from the Don Valley Stadium, where it had all begun for the young Ennis a decade-and-a-half earlier.

The javelin that had proved her undoing in the 2011 world championships was worked on twice a week by former world, Commonwealth and European medallist Mick Hill, at his base at Leeds Metropolitan University.

Hill identified that the problems in Daegu were created by the fact that Ennis naturally leant to the right as she approached the line, which diminished power and distance. To rectify it, Ennis was advised to look over her left shoulder as she threw the javelin, which would naturally straighten her stance. Two sessions a week of that redefined throwing position and a more speed-efficient run-up helped her overcome the problem in time for the Olympics.

As well as an intense training programme, she also had numerous media and sponsorship responsibilities, but given the prize at stake, she was conscious that those extra-curricular activities were managed tightly and never jeopardised her training and rest time.

Then there were the competitions, when early-season form was established. No event was too small, like the sparsely-attended Yorkshire Championships at the Dorothy Hyman Stadium in Cudworth, Barnsley, in early 2012, which was the first chance to put her new javelin technique into practice.

Ennis also bravely returned to Gotzis, in Austria, just two months before the start of London 2012. Any fears that lightning might strike twice were banished when she won the meeting, and broke Denise Lewis's 12-year-old British record in the process. Ennis was as ready as she could have been. All that had gone before, the heartache, the despair, the titles, the unbridled joy, all pointed to one thing.

****

Anyone who was fortunate enough to be in London's Olympic Stadium on the evening of Saturday, August 4, 2012, will never forget it. Nor will the millions who watched a magical night unfold on their television screens. For Jessica Ennis, Mo Farah and Greg Rutherford who produced three of the greatest highlights of even that spectacular summer, it was the night when they entered British sporting lore.

Twenty-five gold medals were up for grabs on the middle Saturday of London 2012, but the three that were won inside 45 minutes in a bouncing Olympic Stadium will go down as the best.

For Sheffield's Ennis, the final event of the heptathlon – the 800m - needed to be nothing more than a couple of victory laps. Eighty-thousand people had filled the Olympic Stadium for the coronation of the queen of the track and she would have been cheered with every stride no matter what she did. But great champions are natural winners and Ennis wanted to go out on a high. She wanted to complete her victory with another personal best and give the crowd who had roared her on from the very first moment she had been welcomed into the arena the previous day, further cause for celebration.

The noise that greeted her on to the start line was as deafening as it had been at any time over the previous two days of competition. It was shortly after 8.30 and darkness had descended over the capital.

Having come so far and got so close to her destiny, nothing was going to stop Ennis now. Instead of settling into the pack and letting her rivals, who had silver and bronze medals to challenge for, set the pace, Ennis burst to the front and dictated the tempo. For the first 400 metres she had no equal, and at the bell that signified the last lap she had the lead. If people wanted to beat her, they would have to run themselves into the ground to do so. Germany's Lilli Schwarzkopf, who was sixth before the 800m and hoping to force her way into the medals, ran past her on the back straight, as did the rangy Tatyana Chernova followed by Canada's Jessica Zelinka.

But as Ennis raced off the final bend on to the home straight and into the final 100 metres of her epic heptathlon, the queen of British athletics muscled her way to front again.

Even after eight years of international competition. Even after the last four years of immeasurable highs and lows. Even after two days of intense Olympic competition, Ennis still had more to give. She sprinted down the home straight, stretching her lead further and further, breaking the spirit of her opponents one last time as she underlined her status as the finest female multi-eventer on the planet.

As she crossed the line to spine-tingling roars from the crowd, television and still cameras captured what would become one of the most indelible images of London 2012: Ennis, arms outstretched, her face holding in the emotions as long as she could before the first strains of relief and delight crept onto her face. The enormity of her accomplishment, achieved in front of an adoring public washed over her as her hands dropped to her knees.

Ennis had achieved her lifelong ambition, doing so with a British record points total of 6,955. She was an Olympic gold medallist and there was no worthier champion. After thrilling the crowd she embarked on her triumphant lap of honour, joined, in the great tradition of multi-discipline events, by the 31 other athletes who had completed athletics' most exacting test. When she had absorbed every last possible image of an unforgettable occasion, she left the stage for Farah and Rutherford to turn a memorable night for British athletics into a momentous, ground-breaking one.

Later that night, the coronation she had scarcely dared to dream about for fear it may jinx it, came to reality as she jumped on to the top step of the podium, waving ecstatically and gratefully to a crowd that could hardly believe what they had witnessed. Tears rolled down her face as the union flag was hoist to the top of its pole and the national anthem saluted her accomplishment.

It was close to midnight by the time she addressed the victory in the medallists' press conference in the bowels of the Olympic Stadium. It was a grey, windowless room, hardly a befitting stage for a victory speech. It was not until the following day that Ennis could finally articulate the enormity of what she had achieved.

"It was a mix of everything," began Ennis, in reference to her reaction as she crossed the line in the 800m. "Missing Beijing and the disappointment of Daegu. There has been so much pressure on me, but I have had so much support. Everyone expected me to win. I had a few moments at home worrying and wondering if it would all go the way I wanted it to...or if everything would fall apart.

"There was a huge amount of pressure but it was a unique position I was in and I wanted to make the most of that. I came into the competition in good shape, the best shape of my life. I had the belief that I could do it."

That she did, in truly dominant, awe-inspiring style.

5. THE BROWNLEE BROTHERS

Alistair Brownlee had a smile on his face as he crouched into a diving position on the start line of the Olympic triathlon of London 2012. This was actually fun to him. The choppy, icy waters of the Serpentine Lake in Hyde Park held no fears for the 24-year-old Yorkshireman. This was the culmination of years of hard work and Brownlee was the red-hot favourite to become Britain's first Olympic champion in triathlon, which had only been part of the programme since the Sydney Games of 2000.

Yet the expectation that had drowned out British stars like Mark Cavendish and Rebecca Adlington earlier in the London Games would not consume the home hope in the triathlon. If anything, Alistair Brownlee was revelling in it. This was his time, his destiny, and he was determined to enjoy it.

What gave him so much pleasure was his confidence. He had arrived at the biggest day of his life in the shape of his life. Not even an Achilles injury suffered at the start of the year had derailed him on his course to Olympic fulfilment. The injury had not panicked him. He even accelerated the recovery time by having a pool built into his back garden so he could aqua-jog in order to get back on the roads around his home quicker. He knew if he performed to the best of his abilities, nobody could catch him.

If he let anything slip in the 1.5km swim through the Serpentine, the 43km bike ride through Hyde Park and the regal surroundings of royal London, or the 10km run to the finish line, then there were only a handful of the 55 starters who could capitalise on such ill-timed misfortune and deny him gold.

One of the triathletes who could beat him and snatch gold stood to his left on the starting jetty on that mild late morning of Tuesday, August 7, 2012. Jonny Brownlee felt the tension, even if his brother didn't. This was a first Olympics for the 22-year-old. He was the reigning world sprint champion, the man ranked the second best triathlete in the world, but he wasn't even the best in his own home.

Alistair was the undisputed king, hoping for an Olympic coronation in front of his adoring public. Jonny, his brother, was the ace up his sleeve. Triathlon is historically an individual sport, with teamwork between compatriots at certain times of the race serving only to aid the team leader who will then run for glory down the finishing straight.

Before Alistair emerged on the international scene in 2008, finishing third in an ITU World Series leg in Madrid to seal a spot in the British squad for the Beijing Olympics that year, triathletes had invariably trained 25 hours a week. By the time of the London Games, the Brownlee brothers had transformed the landscape of the sport. They were the two-headed beast who terrorised all before them, their 35-hours-a-week training regimen making them fitter, stronger and better prepared than any of their rivals.

Pounding the roads and the rugged terrain around the home they shared in the leafy, picture-postcard village of Bramhope on the outskirts of Leeds had helped shape them. The sheer passion they derive from running out of their front door together into the wide open expanses of the Yorkshire Dales or on to the treacherous fells of the neighbouring Chevin Country Park set them apart from the rest. It was something they had been doing as a family since they were boys. It was a hobby that became a profession.

The fact that they were brothers, training and living together, gave them an advantage that the rest of the triathlon world just could not bridge. Burning brightly inside them was that unique bond that siblings share, the pride in seeing a brother do well, but the determination to just be the better man on the day.

If Jonny woke up bright and breezy one winter's morning to train, then Alistair could not live with himself if he allowed sleep to engulf his body and did not follow his brother out into the crisp morning air. Alistair was a better triathlete because he had Jonny pushing him. Jonny was a better triathlete because he had Alistair to chase. As Malcolm Brown, the GB performance director and their mentor down the years, put it, they had the "ability to kick each other up the backside when it was needed".

Together they had revolutionised the world of triathlon, a force of nature that left the rest sweeping leaves on a windy day. Either as a team or as individuals there was no stopping them. Alistair had finished 12th on his Olympic debut in Beijing, at one moment thinking he could actually win a surprise gold before fading into the pack. He was only 20, and the world would not have to wait long to see this phenomenally gifted and tireless individual take the step up.

The world title at the end of the multi-leg world series followed in 2009, complemented by the European title 12 months later. In 2011, when fully fit, he won both the world and continental titles.

Jonny won the world sprint title that year - a race contested over a shorter distance - but in the final months before the Games the younger brother had been the stronger Brownlee. As Alistair rested his strained Achilles tendon in a protective boot, Jonny made hay while the sun shone. He won his first world series events in San Diego and Madrid before normal service was resumed in the final pre-Olympic world series event in Kitzbuhel in June, when Alistair demonstrated in his first major international race of the season that his injury had not undermined his destiny and thus opened the door to his rivals. He won by more

than a minute, with Jonny coming home in second.

With Alistair back and in world-beating form, he took his place on that start line of the London 2012 triathlon as the favourite. Jonny's job in the London Olympic triathlon was not necessarily to try and beat his brother. If the opportunity arose, he could, and would, go for it. But when they sat down and hatched a plan in the late summer of 2011, their mission was to get both of them on the medal podium. Alistair first, Jonny, hopefully second, would be the best way to fulfil an ambition that would be historic. There was no sense in the two working against each other and depriving their family and the British public of a unique, memorable storyline.

That they planned to both be on the podium was no secret. Even the notion of crossing the line together, and so sharing the gold, had been discussed and speculated upon. They did exactly that at a triathlon in Oxfordshire in June - Alistair's first race since injury - taking the plaudits of a crowd moved to tears by such solidarity as they crossed the line together.

Both young Yorkshiremen had said that in the heat of Olympic battle and in a sport with as many intangibles as triathlon, the chance to cross the line together, triumphantly in the Olympic final would be almost impossible. The International Triathlon Union went a step further in the days leading up to the race when they said if the brothers did so they would be disqualified for manufacturing the result.

To their opponents who lined up alongside them on the start line at the Serpentine, the Brownlees represented an irresistible double act that needed beating. Such was the siblings' dominance the fear was that the rest of the 53 athletes were fighting for the one medal that was left. There were a good few athletes in that race who were just happy to be there, but they were outnumbered by those who wanted to rip up an emotive script.

Among them was Kris Gemmell, a 35-year-old New Zealander, who had won the world title in 2002 when the notion of global domination

was unfathomable to Alistair, who was still only competing in British junior triathlons.

In a shot across the bow that echoed the cross-nation teamwork that had gone into denying Mark Cavendish a chance at the gold medal in the men's cycling road race 10 days earlier, the Kiwi issued a warning to the Brownlees that the rest of the world were uniting to hunt them down. The 43km cycle leg, the second stage of the triathlon, which requires more tactical awareness than the swim and the run, was identified as the time when their rivals would gang up on the Yorkshire duo.

"Everyone is aware of who the strong people are in the race," said Gemmell. "It would be stupid for us not to give each other a little help now and then. I'm very friendly with other people from other nations and we've talked about this. We know what's going on and it will be something we will be able to rely on.

"I hope everyone understands that this is not a conspiracy against the Brownlee brothers.

Everybody knows that they're good."

"They're obviously worried about what we can do," was Alistair's counter-attack when he learned of Gemmell's comments and their rivals' plan.

"All we can do is go out and try our best, and to be honest, doing that would be more high risk for them than it is for us. We just have to go out and do what we always do.

"At the end of the day, they know that when they get to the end of the bike they have to have a lot fresher legs than me or be in front of both of us in the race. So if they want to try it, let them."

An area of perceived weakness in the Brownlee make-up is their swimming. So strong are the two brothers, particularly Alistair, in the cycle and running stages, that the fact that they don't usually leave the water at the front of the pack gave the rest of the field a glimmer of hope.

And the swim leg of a triathlon can be a violent part of the race, with 55 competitors all in the water at the same time, cutting a swathe to the next buoy and doing everything necessary to get to the front. That can mean kicking opponents under the water, grabbing their shoulders from behind to tug them back, or the occasional punch to the body of a leading contender.

The Brownlee brothers were mindful not to get caught in the middle of the bunch, when hopes of gold could disappear amid a waterfall of flying limbs. As they headed out, all 55 converging to the first buoy like a squadron of bombers filling a blue sky, Alistair and Jonny Brownlee got themselves among the front-runners early on.

Richard Varga of Slovakia was the pace-setter, cutting through the open water like a propeller blade. Those at the front soon thinned out into single file, with Alistair and Jonny lurking patiently and ominously just a few places off the lead.

For 17 minutes the chill water of the Serpentine

was filled with these brave pugilists embarking on the first phase of the gruelling ordeal that is the triathlon. Wedged in between the two brothers was the rest of the world's best hope of depriving the host nation its fairytale ending. Spain's Javier Gomez was the only man other than Alistair Brownlee to have won a world title in the four-year Olympic cycle to London. The pre-race favourite in Beijing in 2008, he finished fourth after suffering from a stitch.

Later that year he clinched the world title, and did so again in 2010 after Alistair's winter preparation – when a triathlete builds a base of endurance to call upon during the summer season – had been disrupted by a stress fracture of the femur. Gomez had won the European title in Israel in April, 2012, when neither Brownlee had raced, confirming his status as the best of the rest.

Like the Brownlees, though, he did not have the Olympic medal that would seal his place in the pantheon of the all-time greats. While some talked of ganging up on the Brownlees, Gomez went away in the winter of 2011-12 and strengthened his body for the running portion of the race, knowing full well that if he hoped to compete with the brothers, matching them in the run would be the only way. It was a backhanded compliment to the dominance of the Brownlees, who had elevated their sport by changing the practices of seasoned competitors. People were now reacting to keep pace with them, just as Tiger Woods had changed the landscape of golf for ever, by working harder and being stronger than any other player.

Gomez was a veteran by comparison to his younger rivals, and at 29, no doubt conscious that London 2012 was his last shot at Olympic glory. Together with the Brownlees, Varga, Italy's Alessandro Fabian and Russia's Ivan Vasiliev, Gomez began to put distance between himself and the chasing pack. No longer did the swimmers outside the pacesetters have to swim through a person's slipstream.

Right arm over left the Brownlees kept pace with the leaders, conscious of the fact that with their strongest disciplines to come, their chance of glory would be increased with a strong swim.

Towards dry land they swam, the bright blue surface of the transition area on to which the main grandstand cast a shadow, getting closer with every stroke. Varga was the first to plant his feet on the ground in a time of 16 minutes 56 seconds. Little did anyone know but Varga was the Brownlee brothers' secret weapon. If their rivals were going to work together to neutralise the British brothers, then Alistair and Jonny had been a step ahead all the time.

The Slovakian, at 23, had grown up in the same era of triathlon as the Brownlees, attending the same age-group events and travelling the world together as young adventurers blessed to be doing a sport they loved. He was also a terrific swimmer and in the two months leading up to the Games, had lived and trained with the Yorkshiremen, first at their home in Leeds, and then for an entire month at their high-altitude training camp in St Moritz, Switzerland.

Together with Stuart Hayes, the 33-year-old British journeyman who was the third and final member of the home Olympic team, they had trained together, bonded, plotted and schemed how they would tackle the Olympics.

The selection of Hayes by the British team had been controversial. The Londoner was 46th in the world at the time, and yet was chosen ahead of Will Clarke and Tim Don, who at No 12 and No 13 respectively, were arguably better candidates to challenge for the medals. Hayes was selected to serve as a domestique for the Brownlees, a support athlete, with the expressed aim of doing the hard work at the front of the bunch in the cycle race to stretch the field for the Brownlees to decimate in the run. It was a move that was wholeheartedly welcomed by the brothers, particularly Alistair, who saw it as an emphatic statement by the home team that they were going for gold by giving him the necessary tools to claim victory.

Hayes was among the chasing pack some 15 seconds behind when he entered transition after the swim. Jonny Brownlee had exited the water in fourth place in a time of 17 minutes 02 seconds. Gomez and Fabian were ahead of him, with Russian Vasiliev tucked in behind and Alistair Brownlee the last of the six leaders to emerge in a time of 17 minutes 04 seconds.

The transition stalls of the two brothers were situated next to each other, down the far end of the right-hand row that ran parallel with the finish line. Thoughts of that glorious finishing straight just a few feet away were banished from the mind almost instantly with another hour and a half's racing still to be negotiated.

As the two brothers hurriedly finished peeling off their dripping wetsuits that they had already begun to remove the second they exited the water, Jonny quickly glanced at his brother. No words were spoken but there was a collective acknowledgement that the swimming leg had gone as well as could have been expected.

Maybe it was the look to his elder brother for assurance, maybe it was the nerves, or maybe it was the adrenalin pumping so fast around his body that prompted a mistake by the younger Brownlee that left his hopes in

jeopardy.

As they sprinted with their bikes at their side of the blue surface before mounting them and hurrying in pursuit of Gomez - who had executed the transition faultlessly - Jonny was perceived by the judging panel to have committed a triathlon sin.

Almost impossible to detect by an enraptured crowd who were completely embroiled in the dynamic of the race from their position overlooking the action, the 22-year-old had been guilty of mounting his bike too early in transition and would have to serve a 15-second penalty before the end of the race.

It was a pedantic ruling, but a law nonetheless, and something that should not be broken. It was also the first time Jonny Brownlee had ever been penalised for it.

He was unaware of the discrepancy as he set off after Gomez. The lead group that had exited the water became five as the Russian Vasiliev was dropped. On the first two of seven laps - which encompassed a dash out of the park, past Hyde Park Corner, up Constitution Hill before doubling back on itself in front of Buckingham Palace and returning to the park - the breakaway group opened up a 20-second lead.

Alistair and Jonny Brownlee, together with Gomez, were the driving force, taking it in turns to lead off the front, with Fabian and Varga busting a gut to stay in touch. Although after the second lap they were swallowed up by the chase group, the front five had sapped energy out of those that had headed off in hot pursuit.

When five became 22, Stuart Hayes began to earn his corn. With victory not his priority, he hit the front and began to dictate the pace. Each time the triathletes came through transition to start another lap, Hayes was the man leading the way, with Alistair and Jonny both stuck to his back wheel.

Twice during the middle portion of the cycling leg, Alistair pulled off the front and stretched the field again, making the chasing pack work

harder and harder to match the inexorable pace built up over years and years of cycling around his Yorkshire home. On each occasion that he was sucked back, Hayes took up the running once more. Conversation between the three Britons was brief and never more than an encouraging word here, or a direction there, until news of Jonny's penalty reached the trio.

"I heard them call it on No 31 and I thought Alistair's got a penalty, what an idiot," said Jonny after the race. "I didn't realise I'd done anything wrong. Then I looked down at my arm and realised I was the No 31. My first thought was 'that's a shame, I'll have to run even faster now and that might make it interesting'."

If anything it served to heighten the drama. Jonny Brownlee could take the 15-second time penalty at any time, with the penalty box situated just out of view of the main grandstand before the start-finish straight which they would still be cycling and running through another five times.

If Jonny was panicked, he didn't look it, remaining composed and at the edge of his pain threshold throughout. Alistair was angry at the penalty, not just because it had been meted out to his brother, but because pernickety rules serve only to detract from the pure basic skill of racing.

He did not let that anger cloud his judgment. By now the wheels in Alistair's mind were spinning just as frantically as his bicycle wheels. Alistair, an intelligent young man who had taught himself further maths, was now doing the sums in his mind as to how he could best serve his brother and fulfil his own ambition.

"I was thinking about what I could possibly do to alleviate it tactically," said the 24-year-old. "If I could go as hard as I could and only take Jonny with me then maybe he can come back through the field."

In the final laps of the cycling leg, when Hayes continued to stretch the field and keep the Brownlees on schedule, the younger brother

opted against taking his penalty, with the bunch at the front too congested with challengers.

When they dismounted the bikes at the second transition, Jonny was cautious not to do anything that might again give the rule-makers cause to wield their authority. He was motion-perfect as he ran to his stall, hooked up his bike, removed his helmet and put on his running shoes.

When he regained race pace, he did so as one of only four men at the front, with his brother, Javier Gomez and Vincent Luis of France. Hayes, his mission accomplished in the cycling phase, was absorbed by the pack. Just as quickly as the four dropped the rest of the field after a swift transition, Luis was dropped by the best three triathletes in the world as Alistair Brownlee, Javier Gomez and Jonny Brownlee, began to build an advantage. As they ran past

the crowd assembled on the opposite side of the Serpentine, chants of 'Brownlee, Brownlee,' reverberated around Hyde Park and spurred the brothers to run even faster.

Alistair, his back bolt-upright a la sprint star Michael Johnson in the 1990s, was always in the lead, but Gomez refused to be shaken and would not allow the Brownlee brothers to make it a procession. The three of them set a relentless pace, making a mockery of the 75 minutes of torture they had just put their bodies through.

At 5km, half-distance and after two of four laps, the trio had established a 27-second gap on the chasing pack. But it was then that Jonny began to get dropped by the front two. Alistair was still looking comfortable, and Gomez unrelenting in his pursuit, but as they weaved their way through the park for a third time, Jonny began to show the first signs of mental and physical fatigue.

The two in front were now disappearing from sight at every corner and with only one last chance to take the penalty, he had to take his medicine and hope against hope that he was not caught. Jonny peeled off the track and into a painted square off the right-hand side that put him face-to-face with a giant clock that filled his vision. The yellow numbers began to tick down.

Fifteen seconds, 14, 13, 12 - Jonny looked anxious, unable to jog up and down on the spot to keep his body warm because it violated the penalty.

Eleven seconds, ten, nine, eight - Alistair and Gomez were now through the start-finish line for the penultimate time, the race between just the two of them.

Seven seconds, six, five - a quick look behind him but no-one there save for a crowd holding its breath.

Four seconds, three, two – the chasing pack eating into his advantage all the time.

One second, and away he went. "The longest 15 seconds of my life," Jonny said later.

Off he ran out of the shadows and darkness of the penalty box and into the light of hope, stumbling as he did so, but maintaining his footwork. His face was expressionless but his mind was racing with relief and the prospect of glory.

Up ahead, Alistair still led Gomez. He had helped his brother by stretching the field with his powerful running honed on the fells he negotiated as a schoolboy, and now he was free to run for victory himself. The Spaniard had surprised him with his stamina and his will to win, but Alistair had one last hand to play as they entered the 10th and final kilometre of the run.

"I had a very fast 800m-1,000m in me. I was pretty comfortable, as long as he didn't stick with me," said Alistair. His second kick crushed Gomez. The Spaniard had nothing left to respond with as Alistair, with all the energy of a fresh-legged middle-distance runner, sprinted away from his doughty rival.

The last 200 metres was a victory procession as the crowd rose to their feet to welcome their new Olympic champion on to the blue carpet. Where previously he had stayed straight and continued running through transition, this time, he veered off right, the finish line in sight just 100 metres away.

The crowd were going ballistic in support of their hero. Alistair had enough time to run towards the crowd and grab a Union flag from a spectator. He draped it around his shoulders as he had done with a Yorkshire flag 12 months earlier when he won in Hyde Park, and, arms outstretched, pointed to the blue sky above London, his face a picture of elation and relief.

He looked over his shoulder to see Gomez running on to the blue track some 150 metres away. Victory was Alistair Brownlee's, the Olympic title was his, and he was determined to milk it for all it was worth. The smile that had lit up his face on the start line an hour-and-three-quarters earlier returned as he blew a kiss of thanks to the crowd and walked over the line, grabbing the tape triumphantly as he did so.

As the camera flashes went off, he dropped to the floor, exhausted. Gomez was not far behind. What a run it had been from the Spaniard who ensured the Olympic final got the maximum performance out of its champion.

Gomez was 11 seconds behind Alistair who had completed the triathlon in one hour 45 minutes 25 seconds. Alistair's 10k time of 29 minutes 07 seconds was only one minute 23 seconds slower than the time Mo Farah clocked in the Olympic Stadium three days earlier when he won a thrilling gold in the 10,000m. But Farah had not swum 1.5km or cycled 43km beforehand, nor had he stopped running to walk over the line.

The crowd were still on their feet 20 seconds after Gomez had finished to cheer home Jonny

Brownlee, who had absorbed the penalty and won the nation's hearts with a bronze-medal performance. That he finished 20 seconds behind Gomez removed any doubt that the penalty had denied him a silver. Gomez had been the second best triathlete that day. Jonny finished 18 seconds ahead of David Hauss of France.

Jonny and Alistair embraced. Brothers united, their golden mission accomplished, the country's latest heroes. In winning gold and bronze, the Brownlee brothers had become the first British siblings to win medals in an individual sport since 1900, the year of the second Olympics in Paris, when Hugh Doherty won gold in the tennis men's singles and brother Reginald took bronze.

But this Olympic triathlon of 2012 was not only historic, it was epic, and the drama would not end at the finish. Ten minutes after crossing the line, when celebrations should have been jubilant and the never-ending media interviews self-aggrandising, Jonny Brownlee crumpled to the floor.

The young Yorkshireman was exhausted, having run himself into the ground to win an Olympic bronze medal.

"After the finish I collapsed. I felt awful as I crossed the line. It was quite hot out there," said Jonny. "I got into the tent afterwards and felt worse and worse. I overheated and I collapsed. That's part of triathlon, it's a hard sport. Alistair had his turn two years ago and now it was mine."

Two years earlier, one of the few bumps on the road to Olympic glory had seen Alistair collapse at the Hyde Park triathlon. His mother, Cath, a doctor, sprang from the temporary grandstand and rushed down the home straight to the aid of her stricken son.

Her entrance this time was less dramatic but the concern was still there as she rushed to her younger son's side. While Jonny was wrapped in towels and covered in ice, a hush descended over the small corner of Hyde Park where moments earlier such a fantastic, emotional finale had unravelled.

The medal ceremony, scheduled to start within an hour of the race concluding, was pushed back 10 minutes, then another 10 minutes.

Jonny's mother attended to him, along with the medical staff, under a shaded area of the grandstand, as far away from concerned, inquisitive eyes as possible. The calmest person the whole time he was laid out was his brother Alistair, who gave the well-being of his sibling barely a moment's thought.

Dressed in his Team GB tracksuit, Alistair laughed and joked with members of the British team and faces he knew, taking the occasional pat on the back of congratulations with gratitude and a warm smile. Two men he sought out were team-mate Stuart Hayes and Slovakian Richard Varga, the selfless duo he and his brother had trained rigorously with in the two months leading up to the Olympics, whose sacrifices had helped put the Brownlees on the podium.

For the majority of the time Jonny was being tended to, Alistair leant on a railing, his hands folded neatly together as if this was any other day. There was the occasional glance in his brother's direction, but it was almost as if to say: "Come on Bruv, you're stealing my moment."

Deep down, Alistair knew Jonny would all right. And Jonny, too, knew he would be ok. Triathletes collapsing at the end of a race is not uncommon, given what they have put their body through in the previous two hours.

The ordeal lasted all of 45 minutes, before Jonny was finally brought round and placed in a wheelchair. Then the two history boys began to slalom their way through the media interviews. Jonny met the press pack sitting in a wheelchair, no doubt a little sheepish that in his moment of triumph he had been reduced to being unable to stand.

That he had collapsed merely highlighted the lengths these young Yorkshiremen would go to achieve their goals, and heightened the sense of awe with which they were applauded.

When the medal ceremony finally took place back out on the home straight and in front of their mother, Cath, and father, Keith, and a packed main grandstand, the big brother in Alistair returned to the fore. After jumping on to the top step of the podium, his teeth biting into his bottom lip as he let out a triumphant roar, Alistair looked at his medal and turned for the national anthem.

As the first notes of "God Save the Queen" rang out big brother turned to little brother, for whom the colour had returned to the cheeks but the legs were still a little shaky, and mouthed the words: "Are you OK?"

It was a subtle, deeply moving moment that summed up perfectly the brothers' bond.

"I'm immensely proud that my brother got bronze," said Alistair an hour later in his press conference, some three hours after he had won gold. "We made no secret of the fact that we wanted to get two of us on the podium and that's not an easy thing to do considering this country has never won a medal in this sport before, and all the things that can go wrong in a triathlon. For one of us to take a penalty as well."

Of his own accomplishment, Olympic champion Alistair Brownlee – who had been running, swimming and cycling from an early age - was the picture of contentment.

"I've got hundreds of emotions: happy, excited, overwhelmed – a bit of relief in there as well," he said. "Obviously coming into a home Olympics as favourite has been tough. We had a strategy to try and distance ourselves from the Olympics a bit. That was difficult to do. But it (the race) was fantastic. Everything went right, apart from Jonny's penalty, and we couldn't have asked for anything more.

"We gave it everything and it shows the strength of training together, pushing each other on all the time, and the relationship that we have."

Brothers in arms, who had grown up together in West Yorkshire, trained together, lived together, they were now Olympic heroes together.

6. NICOLA ADAMS

There is no Olympic sport quite like boxing to provide the launch pad for a superstar. Through history, many a great of the professional ring has buried deep within his roots the once innocent desire to fight for nothing more than the opportunity to hang a chunk of gold around his neck.

Muhammad Ali in Rome, Sugar Ray Leonard in Montreal and Lennox Lewis in Seoul are just three of the men to have arrived at an Olympic Games as a promising hopeful, only to depart the scene a few days later as a name on the lips of sports fans the world over, and a future champion and king of his era and division. The greatest show on earth provides a natural spotlight for amateur prospects to punch their way into fame and fortune.

By the time of London 2012, the British boxing scene was in need of a new hero. Not since Ricky Hatton or Joe Calzaghe had there been a warrior for the public to huddle round their television sets and get behind. The fight game in Britain was trudging along in near embarrassment and shame. Every time it put its head above the parapet into the national sporting conscience, it did so only to smear its proud name further. Headline acts like David Haye and Derek Chisora had become farcical characters after their public tussle in a post-fight press conference following Chisora's defeat to Vitali Klitschko in Munich in February. Audley Harrison, once an Olympic champion himself, had only lurched from one disappointment to another in the professional sport.

Even Amir Khan and James DeGale, the last great British hopes to burst forth from the Olympic arena, had yet to truly fulfil their potential in the paid ranks. Carl Froch was the closest thing to a Hatton or a Calzaghe, but the valiant battles he fought on either side of the Atlantic were done largely out of the public eye. A vacuum had been created, space for someone to punch their way through and remind the British public that when at its best, boxing and its protagonists can provide some of the greatest moments and champions in sport.

The person who accomplished that at London 2012 was someone for whom the deeds of Ali and Leonard as Olympic amateurs still resonated. That the person who helped reignite the British public's interest in boxing was a woman, and a Yorkshire woman to boot, was one of the most historic and uplifting storylines of the Games.

In the space of three thrilling performances over four days, 29-year-old Nicola Adams of Leeds became a national superstar. She had the quick wit and the radiant smile of a great entertainer. And she could box too, as she proved in those three one-sided fights in the emotionally charged ExCel Arena on the Thames Docklands.

Not only that, but Adams became an icon for the relatively young sport of women's boxing. Prior to London, women's involvement in boxing was viewed with scepticism; the fairer sex should not be encouraged to fight. Ever since she had first laced up a pair of boxing gloves at Sharky's gym near her home in Burmantofts, Leeds, Adams had been venturing into a sport that for women had little future, and no scope for the kind of exposure she would enjoy at the Olympics 17 years later.

"I remember her coming in at the age of 12 and I saw the potential was there straight away," said Leroy "Sharky" Brown of that first day Adams stepped into his club. "For a young girl to walk into the gym and take an interest in boxing was pretty much unheard of back then. She was one of the first girls in Leeds to do it. Where she led, others followed."

Adams took up boxing not to be the trailblazer she would become, but because she was inspired to do so by sitting with her father and watching the fights of Ali and Leonard. As her father sat enthralled in front of the television, Adams would dance around the living room, shadow boxing to the rhythm of her heroes. Even then, distant dreams of being a gold medallist were being formed in the young girl's mind, even though its acceptance as an Olympic sport never looked likely.

In spite of that, as she fought her way through the junior and senior ranks of women's amateur boxing, her belief that one day she would fight at the Olympics and follow in the footsteps of her heroes never wavered. Throughout all the controversies and dramas in the men's professional game, and through the many knock-backs women's boxing received when it tried to gain acceptance not only into the Games programme but also into the general sporting domain, Adams's belief in the inherent good of the sport she loved never died.

She was 13 when she first fought in a boxing ring. She won, but such was the paucity of teenage girls boxing in 1995, that she had to wait another four years for her next fight. By then, the British Amateur Boxing Association had sanctioned the first bout for girls. It generated a media storm, with there being little appetite for women in the country to go down the same route that other nations were tentatively exploring.

The first European Cup of women's amateur boxing would not take place until 1999, with the first world championship two years later. By then, Adams had graduated to national honours, and in a prescient nod to the landmark feat she would accomplish 11 years later, she became the first woman to represent England in an amateur women's boxing bout in 2001.

Within two years there were enough women boxers to stage an English championship.

Adams won the national title in the inaugural event, the first of three in succession and four in total. Like the honour-laden pasts of the men she aspired to emulate, Adams was racking up the achievements. National accolades soon became international kudos as Adams progressed to the continental arena in 2007. Where only victories had fed her insatiable appetite at home, against more experienced fighters in Europe and the wider world, Adams had to learn how to deal with defeat.

She lost the respective finals of the European and world championships in Denmark in 2007 and in China the following year. She fought both of those in the 54kg bantamweight category, before taking the decision in 2010 to drop down to the 51kg flyweight division.

That choice was made after a 12 months that proved both inspirational and devastating for a fighter who was now in her mid-20s. In June, 2009, she slipped down the stairs at her home in Leeds and broke a bone in her back. Adams spent three months laid in her bed, wondering if her career was over. When news came later that summer that women would at last be fighting for Olympic gold in the forthcoming Games, Adams lay on her shattered spine petrified that fate had cruelly robbed her of the chance to do what she had long dreamt of doing.

"I was thinking to myself 'am I going to be able to go from not being able to do one sit-up to actually winning gold?'" she would later say.

But like all great champions, she found the inner strength to pick herself up off the canvas. Her mother Dee was a constant source of support and encouragement during such a trying time. By the start of 2010 Adams was back in the ring, and now actively encouraged by the British Amateur Boxing Association who had moved the women's team into the Team GB headquarters at Sheffield's English Institute of Sport. Pictures of Britain's former Olympic medallists hung from the walls. The faces of Alan Minter, Richie Woodhall, Audley Harrison and others from the past provided a constant reminder to the new men and women of British amateur boxing of just what could be achieved.

What the squad base in Sheffield gave Adams was that long sought-after sense of belonging. She had ploughed a lone furrow for much of her boxing career, reliant on the financial support of her family allied to bit-part acting jobs and work on a building site. Now she was lottery funded and in touching distance of anything she needed to help her golden quest, be it dietary advice, a massage after a tough day's training, or the counsel of a sports psychologist. She even sparred with the men to increase her strength and speed.

Such home comforts helped shape the fighter she would become. A year after nearly seeing her career come crashing down around her following an innocuous slip, Adams was back in the world championship final, this time in Barbados.

She lost, to Chinese flyweight Ren Cancan, in what was the first act in a compelling two-year narrative between the two fighters. But she had at least proved to herself that the back injury had been overcome and that she still had the ability to go the distance in a major championship.

In 2011 Adams, who split her time between training at the EIS and at the gym of Brendan and Dominic Ingle, claimed her first major international accolade by defeating home favourite Karolina Michalczuk to win the European title in Poland. It was a significant breakthrough heading into Olympic year.

But first up was the small matter of a world championship in Qinhuangdao, China, in May, in which advancing to the quarter-final would book her spot in the historic first women's boxing tournament at the Olympics later in the summer. It was a double incentive and something she achieved without allowing the merest hint of a potential upset to enter her mind.

Once again she reached the final and once again she met Cancan, who this time had the home crowd in her corner. Adams was beaten for the second time, making it three world championship finals in succession that she had lost. Any question marks over her ability to deliver when it mattered most were tempered somewhat by her belief that the 14-11 margin with which Cancan outpointed her owed much to the home crowd influencing the judges.

Adams left China with mixed emotions over yet another silver medal, but at least buoyed that she had narrowed the gap on Cancan. In London the full force of the home crowd would be in her corner, and she was determined to use that to her advantage.

She had also beaten her great nemesis at the lower-profile Strandja Cup in Bulgaria earlier that year, which gave her the confidence that she had at least on one occasion proved more than a match for the world No 1.

Adams was one of three Britons among 36 boxers from 23 nations embarking on the first women's Olympic boxing tournament. Savannah Marshall and Natasha Jonas were Adams's compatriots and the three of them stood on the threshold of history.

The first women's bout was held on Sunday, August 5, between Russia's Elena Savelyeva and Hye Song Kim of North Korea, and was won by the Russian. The first Briton to fight was 28-year-old Jonas of Liverpool who comfortably outpointed Quanitta Underwood of the United States in her first bout in the 60kg category.

Adams, the No 2 seed, was given a bye into the last eight of the flyweight competition. When she finally got the chance to make her mark on the second day, the true potential of this beaming, bonny lass from Leeds was quickly realised.

Having boxed to little acclaim for much of her career, that first walk out from under the structured steelwork of the stands into the darkened arena could have proven an overwhelming experience for Adams, or any of the British girls. But ever since she had stepped into a ring for the first time all those years ago,

Adams had dreamt of this moment. And she was not going to let noise like she had never experienced before, generated by 10,000 fans inside the little black hole of the ExCel Arena's south hall, overwhelm her.

Far from it, Adams actually rose to the occasion and revelled in it as she walked towards her corner for her quarter-final bout with Stoyka Petrova of Bulgaria, a former European bronze medallist and her country's only representative in the women's boxing tournament.

Adams went straight after Petrova from the first bell of a contest that would last for four, two-minute rounds with the five judges at ringside counting the telling blows that would decide the winner on points. Switching stances from orthodox to southpaw, and keeping her hands low - such was the confidence that her nimble footwork would get her out of trouble - Adams danced around the ring causing the Bulgarian all manner of problems. A series of left-right combinations found their range and the Yorkshire woman also did damage with body shots.

But after two rounds the judges had not been as enamoured by her performance as many at ringside, giving her only a two-point lead at 5-3. In previous Olympics, scoring during the rounds was visible on the scoreboard as points accumulated ticked over for everyone in the auditorium to see. At London 2012, television viewers and those inside the venue did not know the scores until the end of each round when they flashed up on the screens, which invariably led to either cheers of delight that their fighter was in front, or moans of derision at a losing score.

Adams, though, would not be deterred and in the penultimate round, she started to move away on points from Petrova, who was being overwhelmed by the sprightliness of her opponent, her range and her guile. Even though she only had to ensure she was not caught by a sucker punch, Adams remained on the offensive in the fourth and final round, opening with a right to the face that rocked

Petrova on her heels, before finishing the bout with another flurry of left and right shots to the head.

The final scoreline of 16-7 arguably should have been wider, but among the many certainties from that eight minutes of pure aggression, was that here was a woman at home in a boxing ring on the biggest stage in the amateur sport. Such was the conviction with which she defeated Petrova and the ease at which she found herself in such surroundings, Adams even managed to entertain the crowd with a quick Ali shuffle, a dance of the feet in homage to one of her heroes.

"I had to get an Ali shuffle in there, it had to be done," she said afterwards. "I've watched so many of his fights and videos that I had to get a cheeky one in there. I enjoyed every moment of it, like I said I would. It's a once-in-a-lifetime experience to just soak up the atmosphere and enjoy every minute. I'm a bit of an entertainer, the more the crowd cheer, the more I'll do."

One other certainty was that Adams, after just one win, was an Olympic medallist. In boxing, there is no bronze-medal bout between beaten semi-finalists, which meant that even if she lost her semi-final, Adams would still be adding to Yorkshire's and Britain's medal tally. She stayed at ringside to see if her stablemates Jonas and Marshall could follow in her historic footsteps by assuring themselves of medals.

But where Adams had prospered, the other two Britons found the going a lot tougher. Jonas was up against the top seed, Ireland's Katie Taylor, in the 60kg lightweight category later that afternoon. Ordinarily Jonas would have been the fighter with the greater support, but British fans even in their own arena were out-sung by the Irish supporters. The sheer amount of them and the noise they generated made a mockery of a balloted ticketing system that had come under scrutiny in the build-up. They furiously waved their flags and passionately cheered their fighter with every punch. Taylor won a pulsating fight 26-15 to

the delight of the Irish fans, who created a noise that reached 114 decibels, akin to a thunder clap.

Shortly afterwards, Marshall, who had won the world middleweight title in Qinhuangdao three months earlier and had been the big hope of the three home fighters to be the first British Olympic champion, suffered a surprise quarter-final defeat to Marina Volnova of Kazakhstan. The 21-year-old from Hartlepool froze on the stage Adams had gleefully embraced only two hours earlier.

Suddenly Adams was the last British woman standing. The road to fame and fortune was hers to stride down alone. Blocking her path were two women who had won eight world titles between them.

Ren Cancan had made light work of Elena Savelyeva in the top half of the draw, while India's Mary Kom erred on the side of unscrupulous as she defeated Tunisia's Maroua Rahali to seal her spot in the semi-final against Adams. Kom was guilty of a rabbit punch (to the back of the head) and hitting Rahali after the bell, which indicated a woman who would do anything to reach the Olympic final. Adams knew she had to be wary of such tactics when the two returned to the ring for their semi-final bout on the Wednesday. She also had the greatest of respect for Kom, whose five world titles demanded as much, as did her status as India's leading female boxer.

Once again Adams strode confidently into the ring, the crowd rising to their feet to acclaim a woman who was visibly inspired by the welcome she received. Kom had won her world titles two weights below before stepping up to flyweight to ensure she would be able to compete in the Olympics, given that the 48kg-51kg flyweight division was the lowest weight category.

And it was immediately clear that the Yorkshire woman, who had beaten her in the world championships earlier in the year, would again have too much range and too much speed. Adams worked well behind her jab in the opening round, keeping Kom at the end of her reach before unleashing a damaging left upper cut in the second that helped her move clear on points at 5-2.

Sensing that the third round would be pivotal, Adams increased her tempo and stretched the lead to 8-4. A rabbit punch from Kom in the final round signified a fighter who was running out of options. Adams just had to be sensible and not jeopardise all she had worked for in the previous three rounds and 17 years.

She did not, sealing the fourth round again by a narrow margin which was enough to complete an 11-6 victory. Right on the bell the Leeds starlet once again treated the crowd to the Ali shuffle, something that was quickly becoming her trademark. A star was being born in front of the nation's eyes. Her humility was equally endearing, whether it was in saying that she was doing this to make her mum, Dee, proud, or paying tribute to her vanquished opponent.

"I've got a lot of respect for her," said Adams of Kom. "She boxed her heart out and gave her all. On the day I was just that little bit better. I stuck to the tactics the coaches gave me and worked with that. I've been preparing for this my whole life and I didn't want to do anything silly. I've been training since I was 12 and to think I'm finally here, I'm really happy."

The semi-final win changed bronze into a guaranteed silver, but it was the gold that Adams coveted. Blocking her path to boxing history was, as many had expected, Ren Cancan, who had not been as convincing as Adams in her nervy 10-8 victory over Marlen Esparza of the United States.

It was the final, the moment of destiny that Adams had been working towards the last two-and-a-half years. And this time the boisterous home support were in her corner. As well as she was boxing - and she was performing to devastating effect - she had been emboldened by the crowd that cheered her no matter what. The whole experience was also serving to inspire her.

Adams was growing in stature as the week progressed, looking more and more at home with every passing minute, from the ring walk, to the celebrations, to the interviews that were so much more poised than those she had given in the lead up to the Olympics when often a sheepish grin suggested she didn't know what all the fuss was about.

In the wake of her semi-final win over Mary Kom, Adams met reporters under the steel structure of the stand that was again rocking to the beat of Ireland's Katie Taylor. There she verbally sparred with seasoned boxing journalists who had shared time with the greats of the sport, like the Leonards and Alis who had so inspired her.

"Who's the favourite for tomorrow's final?" came the question. "You tell me," she laughed. "What do you guys think?" Adams was so comfortable it was if she had rehearsed every moment of her Olympic journey a million times.

What she could not anticipate, or allow to disrupt her flow, was Cancan. Twenty-six hours later they were back in the darkness of the ExCel for the biggest fight of their lives. Scheduled for the slightly later time of 4.30 on Thursday, August 9 – both Adams's previous bouts had been at 1.45 – the final of the women's 51kg flyweight final would be a momentous, historic occasion.

The atmosphere inside the 10,000-seater south hall that day was electric. A nervous current burned through all who were there. As had happened on the previous days, Ireland's Taylor would be fighting in the lightweight category straight after Adams, and it was as if half of Ireland had descended on the Docklands area of south east London to cheer her on.

The Irish fans generated so much noise for each of Taylor's fights, that the senses were so heightened that sound became feel. The crowd eruption reverberated around the small arena like a shock of wind in an air tunnel, making hairs stand on end and inducing a lump in the throat. When the Irish chanted "Ole, Ole, Ole, Ole" in unison, it was hard to choke back the tears, such was the emotion that hung in the air.

Even out on the concourse of the vast ExCel Arena, their chants echoed off the high walls. Long after Taylor had outpointed Russia's Sofya Ochigava 10-8 in a ding-dong 60kg final, Irish fans filled the concourse, dancing and celebrating their country's first gold medal as if they had topped the entire medals table. It was a sight to behold and the only thing in the boxing arena that second week of the Games that Nicola Adams did not orchestrate.

As with her opening two bouts, Adams had the reaction of the crowd – which included the Duchess of Cambridge Kate Middleton - in the palm of her hand like a conductor leading a chorus line. Wearing the blue she had sported all week, Adams touched gloves with Cancan, an opponent for whom she had the utmost respect, and commenced the historic eight minutes of Olympic action with only one thought in her mind: victory.

A frenetic opening saw the fighters go toe to toe, with Adams getting the better of one particularly wild exchange on the ropes. When she established the high ground in the centre of the ring, her orthodox stance and left jab kept her in control of the fight as her right occasionally forced its way through the guard to halt Cancan in her tracks.

The slight edge she had gained in the first round became an overwhelming advantage in the second as Adams knocked the top-ranked fighter to the canvas with a left jab flush to the face followed by a right hook that helped the Chinese favourite on her way to the bright blue canvas. In such a short bout one knockdown can be decisive and Adams had seized the advantage. Cancan was given a standing eight count and continued on, but the damage had been done.

She tried in vain to alter the course of the bout in the third round, but the nimble Adams was too fleet of foot to be caught in any serious danger. As she walked back to her stool at the end of the penultimate round, Adams – who had built a 14-5 lead - raised a fist to the crowd in acknowledgement of their support and how on top of the occasion she felt.

Her Olympic destiny was now in sight. Just two more minutes had to be negotiated. Wisely, Adams stayed behind a high guard in the final round, picking her shots selectively as Cancan danced furiously and threw punches wildly to try and create an opening. But it was not to be. The young girl who shadow-boxed to the greats in front of the television, who fearlessly walked into a gym full of boys her own age when she was just 12, had fulfilled her lifetime's ambition and punched her way to a place no other female boxer had gone before.

She even managed a hasty Ali shuffle with seven seconds remaining, one last nod to her great inspiration. When the final bell sounded she was still head down and on the charge, forcing Cancan back as if she were the punchbag at Sparky's gym in Leeds. There was no instantaneous jump for joy when the reality dawned that the fight was over, just a quick walk over to Cancan and one last pat of the gloves between the two combatants.

Then Adams turned to all four corners of the arena and threw a shadow punch in the direction of the crowd, the smile that had radiated from her face all week now brighter than ever. High-fives were traded with the GB coaches in her corner, but there was no over-the-top celebrations between them as Adams removed her headguard and her bandana to reveal her braided hair.

Within a minute the verdict was in and even before her name was announced, the scores flashed up on the screens around the arena and the cheers went up. The first women's boxing champion in Olympic history skipped on the spot in sheer delight as the crowd acclaimed Britain's new boxing hero. She pointed to the three lions on her blue vest as she danced in the centre of the ring and then posed for the cameras. Even Cancan had a smile of acknowledgement on her face. Nothing she could have done in that gold-medal bout could have altered the historic course Adams had set out on.

"It's like a dream come true. I've wanted this all my life, and in front of all this support it's really made my day," she said. "I'm just so happy and overwhelmed with joy right now."

Later on after collecting her gold medal at ringside, to the sheer delight of the 10,000 spectators who had witnessed history in the making, Britain's new ring sensation was able to articulate further how she had overcome her great nemesis on the greatest stage of all.

"I thought it would be a bit closer, but I was just so determined to win that I wasn't going to let her win," she said. "I went in fully focused because if I think I'm going to lose, I will lose. I cannot let that enter my mind. I have to be focused and so confident. There is no other option but to win. I didn't see the knockdown coming, it just happened."

As much as a triumph for herself, Adams, with that cherubic smile and lightning fists, had struck a blow for women's boxing. Doubters had been turned to converts by her masterful performances and ring presence. Adams exuded star quality, and in the space of four days had helped fill the vacuum in a sport searching for a new star.

The importance of her historic first was not lost on the Yorkshire woman. As she addressed the press pack hours after her victory, in a suite bathed in early evening sunshine overlooking the vast Thames Docklands - a rare sight after an afternoon in the intense, dark arena of the ExCel - Adams was very much aware of the important step she had just taken for women's sport.

Asked whether her achievement had answered the questions over the validity of women's boxing, Adams said: "I've not answered that one, the crowd has. They've been absolutely amazing and they've been cheering as much for us as they have for the lads. There's no better place to showcase the sport. I can't believe the support we've had and it's great how Britain has got behind women's boxing.

"I want to see more girls getting into boxing and participating in the sport. When I retire, if

I could see girls wanting to achieve what I have done then that would be an amazing feeling. If young girls see me winning gold and want to get into boxing because of that then I will have achieved everything. To think that girls will now have role models to look up to is great for the sport.

"And if I have any message to them, whether you're doing boxing, or whatever sport, or even if it is just a job you're after, it is that if you work hard you can achieve anything."

Adams not only achieved her lifetime's dream at London 2012, she broke down barriers in the process, doing so in such an inspirational, exciting and entertaining manner that she became one of the icons of the summer Olympics.

7. LUKE CAMPBELL

Luke Campbell was surprised at how anxious he felt. He was about to enter the ring for his Olympic debut. The moment he had worked towards for over a decade and had been waiting patiently for over the last four years was finally here, yet he was a bundle of nervous energy.

By the second stage of the men's bantamweight competition, the 24-year-old should have been settled into his rhythm. Those pre-fight butterflies that were leaping in his stomach as he awaited the call to step out into the arena in the evening session on Wednesday, August 1, should have been behind him.

He should have fought four days earlier in the first round, a nice easy bout to begin his maiden Olympic campaign. A chance to stretch the legs, to test the range, to acclimatise to the atmosphere and get a win tucked under his belt. But as the third seed he had got a bye into the last 16 and instead of that nice straightforward fight he had hoped for, Campbell was preparing for doughty Italian Jahyn Vittorio Parrinello, who could trip up some of the best fighters in the 56kg category on his day.

What exacerbated Campbell's nerves was the pressure on his shoulders. Just as Jessica Ennis carried with her the hopes and expectations of her home city of Sheffield, so Campbell was Hull's great hope for Olympic glory. He was immensely proud of that fact. His home city was a place he held dear to his heart. But that brought with it a determination not to let anybody down. He knew the people of Hull and those family members and friends who had followed and supported him on his journey, were proud of him no matter what. But this was the Olympics. He had already suffered disappointment four years earlier

when he narrowly missed out on selection for Beijing. Now he was finally here, he did not want to suffer heartbreak again. He spent much of those four extra days trying to keep those thoughts out of his mind.

Parrinello was a tricky customer and Campbell had to be sharp mentally and physically. Despite his nerves, the Yorkshireman looked intensely focused as he made his way to the ring for the first time, the 10,000 fans in the ExCel Arena already in fine voice as they chanted 'Team GB' as their man entered the fray.

In early stages the nerves showed. Parrinello already had a win to his name having defeated Namibia's Jonas Matheus in his first bout, and began strongly, dictating the tempo in the first of three, three-minute rounds. But Campbell found his range with a succession of left and rights to eventually tie the round 3-3. The Briton had the crowd on their feet with a crashing left that jolted Parrinello's head back as he took an 8-6 lead going into the final three minutes. And that proved decisive, for although he was still caught by the lively Italian as they traded blows. The judges' 3-3 score was enough to secure Campbell his place in the quarter-final, 11-9 on points.

Campbell's Olympic baptism had been a little too close for comfort, and he was relieved to have prevailed. "Hopefully it gets better as it goes along," was his assessment. "I kept it tidy and kept popping him down the middle. It wasn't my best performance but it was my first fight and my nerves were going. I always tell myself that I won't put pressure on myself and I'll enjoy the occasion, but you can't get away from the pressure. It's about trying to keep calm. Now I've got that first one out of the way hopefully I will get better through the tournament."

****

Luke Campbell took up boxing because he thought it was "cool". He was 13 when he walked off the street in his home city of Hull and into a boxing gym for the first time. The sport was not in the family, but Campbell wanted to win a few trophies to put on the mantelpiece of his family home. The early signs, though, were that honours would be a long way off as Campbell lost six of his first nine fights.

Even that shaky start to life as a schoolboy boxer did not dampen his enthusiasm. The fact that he did not like getting beaten drove him to improve and stick at a sport he was growing to love. There was an inner desire to get better.

Campbell took the decision to move to St Paul's Amateur Boxing Club after his first season and he quickly started progressing. The coach at St Paul's, Mike Bromby, was impressed with what he saw in Campbell, even at that young age. "He was street-wise, even with that angel face," said Bromby. The teenager's balance and movement caught the eye, but more than anything else it was the determination to get better that heartened Bromby. When he progressed to the England junior ranks, Campbell would still return from week-long training camps and head to St Paul's to continue his development further.

"Looking back now I often wonder what was in my head to keep me carrying on and trying so hard," Campbell reflected of those early years. "Because ever since that first day I started boxing I've treated it as a profession; living the life, not cutting corners or cheating, disciplined in everything I did, eating well, not going out late at night, staying away from girls. I was living maybe a bit too intense."

Throughout his teenage years Campbell experienced highs and lows in the junior and senior schoolboy ranks, all of it valuable experience for later life in the ring. There was no question he would do anything else. Boxing was his first love and he was now harbouring dreams of winning Olympic gold.

If he or anyone else needed proof of his burgeoning talent, Campbell delivered it in 2007 when he won the English senior amateur boxing association title. He defended it 12 months later, emphatically so in a 23-1 points destruction of Gareth Smith, setting him up perfectly for the big events to come that year.

****

If his victory over Parrinello was close, Campbell's quarter-final bout with Detelin Dalakliev was even closer. The two had history, and encouragingly for the Yorkshire fighter, it was weighted in his favour as he had beaten the Bulgarian twice in major championships.

He also had the partisan home crowd in his favour, and had got that opening win under his belt, however tentative the performance had been. But Dalakliev, a world champion only three years earlier, would prove even tougher and would require the Hull fighter to dig deeper than ever before to keep his bid for gold on track.

Those nerves that had threatened to engulf him in his first bout were still evident in a cagey opening round as the crowd attempted to lift him with their rhythmic hand clapping. Campbell scored with a couple of long, right hands, his range again working to his advantage. But the wily Dalakliev kept a close guard and smothered the southpaw's advances, retaliating with scoring blows of his own that saw him edge in front at the end of the first round.

There was a tension in the air as Campbell walked out into the middle of the ring for the second round, the crowd in the ExCel Arena acutely aware of just how finely-balanced the contest was. The added incentive of a guaranteed bronze for the winner heightened the drama. Whoever progressed would take home a medal even as a beaten semi-finalist, and Campbell had the chance to become the first Briton out of the 10 fighters at the home Games to qualify for that stage.

In that respect, the quarter-final can be just as edgy as a semi, and so it was proving as

Campbell looked to up the tempo in the middle three minutes. His rangy rights were still landing but in close quarters he was being bullied and the Bulgarian caught him with damaging upper cuts.

The Hull boxer found himself trailing by a point going into the final round. If he was to fulfil his dream, these next three minutes would be crucial. Campbell remained on the attack, but so did Dalakliev. Campbell scored with a couple of left hooks but still the bout was on a knife-edge. Sensing as much, the two warriors went hell for leather in the closing 45 seconds, standing toe to toe in the middle of the ring trading blows. Both men raised their arms at

the bell, more in hope than expectation. There had been little to choose between the two fighters and the outcome would be determined by the judges.

An anxious few minutes passed, with Campbell's Olympic dream now in the hands of someone else. When the result was announced, 16-15 to the Briton, it stirred in Campbell a mixture of relief and elation that he had survived another significant test of his resolve, and had guaranteed a medal.

"It feels fantastic," he said. "I've worked all my life to get to this point, made sacrifices, stayed disciplined, but this makes it all worthwhile. He

was trying to spoil me, holding me a lot, but I just had to keep calm and let the punches go. The right guy won in the end."

****

The battle for the one spot in the bantamweight competition at the Beijing Olympics was between two men, Hull's Luke Campbell and Manchester's Joe Murray. Campbell, now 20, was continuing to fly the flag for the East Riding and St Paul's ABC, but was also spending more time at the GB boxing base at Sheffield's English Institute of Sport.

Murray, equally adept and entrenched in the British system, was the first man to qualify to go to the Far East and the only man the selectors chose to take. It was a devastating blow for Campbell, and when Murray was beaten in the first round in Beijing, it merely added insult to injury that he had not been given the chance to qualify. However, during all of his career in the boxing ring, Campbell had shown he has the mental fortitude to bounce back.

What he did later in 2008 only emphasised that further. Determined not to let the disappointment be the breaking of him, Campbell crossed the M62 for the European Amateur Championships in Liverpool and won gold, defeating a bronze medallist from Beijing along the way. He became the first Briton to win a European title in any division for 47 years, beating Detelin Dalakliev in the final.

It was a career high for Campbell, but as ever in this young man's rise, a peak was quickly followed by a trough. The following year took him to breaking point. The British boxing system changed, different coaches came in, and even though he was only an hour's drive from his home in Hull, Campbell suddenly felt lost in Sheffield.

"The whole of 2009 was a miserable year", he said. "At one point I was looking to get out, I didn't want to do it anymore. Because of the environment I was in, I just didn't like it."

The man to re-energise Campbell was Rob McCracken, a former British middleweight who came in as GB performance director at the end of 2009. "It became enjoyable to train again," said Campbell, whose spirits during that trying period were kept as high as possible by his family and by Mike Bromby at St Paul's. "I felt very confident under the wing of Rob and the coaches there."

As had happened with other Yorkshire champions at London 2012, like Katherine Copeland, Jessica Ennis and Nicola Adams, whose personal nadirs had helped shape them, so the depths Campbell was recovering from provided him with further reason to excel. As Campbell put it: "I'd been to the worst place possible in my career, so what else was I afraid of?"

****

All through the Olympic competition, Luke Campbell's main motivation for glory was to make his son proud. Leo Campbell was only two but had sat in front of the television at the family home in Hull watching his dad fight his way through to the medal rounds of the bantamweight competition. Making his son proud, as well as his home city, was what inspired Campbell every time he set foot in the ring in the ExCel Arena.

By Friday, August 10, he was just two wins away from fulfilling that ambition. He could have settled for the bronze he had already achieved and taken that home to his young boy, but Campbell craved the gold, to make his son as proud as possible. To do that he would need to win the two biggest fights of his life in a little over 24 hours, with the semi-final quickly followed by Saturday's final.

After fighting twice in nine days, the intensity at the medal stage had ratcheted up a notch. If those first two bouts had hammered home just how hard he would have to fight to achieve his dream, then the semi-final would provide Campbell with his safest passage yet. Japan's Satoshi Shimizu was a surprise contender in the last four. He had even been beaten, controversially so, in the second stage, only for the result to be overturned. Shimizu trailed Azerbaijan's Magomed Abdulhamidov by seven points going into the final round, but as his opponent began to tire, Shimizu knocked him to the canvas five times.

The ruling at ringside was that Abdulhamidov had prevailed on points, but Japanese officials argued that he should have been given three warnings for the amount of times he was floored, and therefore disqualified. The International Amateur Boxing Association agreed, and a reprieved Satoshi won his next fight to book a semi-final against Campbell. Considering who was on the opposite side of the draw, Ireland's John Joe Nevin and Cuba's former world champion and gold-medal favourite Lazaro Alvarez, it was at last a favourable tie for the Hull man.

Relatively tall for a bantamweight at five foot nine inches, Campbell was the smaller man in the semi-final against the lanky Shimizu, who had a good two inches on the Briton. Initially the rangy Japanese fighter caused problems with a straight jab that had Campbell on the back foot, but the Hull man is an expert counter-puncher and used his quick footwork to establish angles of attack. The scoring blows were not obvious, but they were plentiful in that opening round, one left to the head in particular getting the 10,000 fans to their feet.

He led 5-2 at the end of the first, the biggest impression he had made yet on the scorecards. The second would be closer, even though Campbell strengthened his grip on the fight by increasing his work-rate. He dominated the centre of the ring and repelled everything that the desperate Japanese fighter could throw at him before picking him off with relative ease.

Going into the final round, Campbell was 11-6 in front. His combinations did the most damage in those closing minutes as the Yorkshire bantamweight sought to close out the contest without allowing the prospect of an upset to enter Shimizu's mind. In a free-scoring round he nearly had Shimizu on the canvas with a right hook as he streaked further ahead, eventually winning 20-11 on points.

Campbell was measured in his assessment of the semi-final, conscious of the fact that it would mean little to him if he did not back it up the following day. "He was more awkward than he looked really," he said. "He was a tough opponent but I prepared well enough and did enough to win." Luke had certainly done Leo proud.

****

Reinvigorated by the new coaching set-up at Sheffield's English Institute of Sport, Luke Campbell won 23 consecutive fights between 2010 and 2011. It was a run of form that confirmed his return to the form of his European title-winning days and it led Rob McCracken, his inspiration in the Steel City, to describe Campbell as the "benchmark" for the rest of the British squad.

Campbell was comfortable again in the state-of-the-art facility. The pictures of former Olympic medallists that adorned the walls of the gym proved an inspiration. When he looked up at the shots of James DeGale, Tony Jeffries and David Price – medallists from Beijing – he was not filled with regret that he had been overlooked four years ago, but determination.

Campbell's time would come, of that he was confident. London was his goal, and the next step to ensuring that was by removing any other bantamweight from the equation and qualifying by rights for the forthcoming Olympics. He was the outstanding amateur in the 56k division in the country but still needed to go to the world championships in Azerbaijan in 2011 and prove that by qualifying for the Games.

"I was saying to myself before I went to the worlds that not only do I really want to qualify for London, I also want to get to a good position," he said. "Because if I'm thinking about winning an Olympic gold I need to start proving myself now."

Campbell needed to win three fights and reach the quarter-finals to qualify for London. Not only did he manage that – defeating former champion Dalakliev along the way - but he reached the final, beating Ireland's John Joe

Nevin on a countback in the semi-final. In the gold-medal bout he met Cuba's Lazaro Alvarez and after starting slowly, left himself too much to do to come back and win gold. It would be a learning curve he was determined to profit from the following year.

A world silver medal was reward enough for a terrific two weeks in Baku. "For me the worlds were about making a statement," he said. "Not necessarily to anyone else, but mainly to myself that I deserve to be up there with the best, beating all the top kids, and that gave me even more confidence to train harder for the Olympics."

****

For his son, for his family, for Mike Bromby and Rob McCracken, for the city and the people of Hull - the list of inspirations for Luke Campbell was endless. He also had the burning desire on the evening of Saturday, August 11, to win Olympic gold for himself, to justify all the hours spent in St Paul's as he grew into a man, and at the EIS as he developed his world-beating technique.

History was also beckoning him. Britain had not won gold in the bantamweight division since Henry Thomas in 1908, the first time London had hosted the Games. And Campbell was determined to follow the groundbreaking path his Yorkshire stablemate Nicola Adams had walked just two days earlier.

Added spice for the final came in the shape of his opponent, John Joe Nevin, who had outpointed Lazaro Alvarez 19-14 in the semi-final. Campbell knew Nevin well. He had beaten him in Azerbaijan the year before but had also lost to him earlier in his career. Campbell has roots in Ireland. His grandfather was Irish boxing champion and some of his family lived in the Emerald Isle and knew the Nevin family. But Campbell believed he had the weapons in his arsenal, and the nous, to beat this familiar foe.

He was, after all, confidently riding the crest of a wave following his comfortable semi-final victory. Campbell may not have exuded the showman qualities of Adams who owned the arena from the second she walked into it, but he had grown into the Olympic tournament, gaining in self-belief with every fighter he overcame.

There was a party atmosphere in the darkened ExCel that evening with both sets of supporters determined to enjoy themselves. The contingent of Irish fans, who had lifted the roof in their support of Katie Taylor earlier in the week, were back. They were outnumbered though by people from Hull, the majority of them decked in white shirts with "Good luck Luke" emblazoned on them. Mike Bromby had made the journey down, as had many of Campbell's family, though his two-year-old son was again in front of the television back at home.

What was witnessed that night was an enthralling Anglo-Irish final, befitting of the stage as it swung one way and then the other. Campbell won the first round after a nervy opening from both fighters. He landed the cleaner shots, with his jab proving effective and his left hook regularly causing problems for the Irishman's orthodox stance.

Back came Nevin in the second round, looking to quickly wipe out the 5-3 deficit. Campbell's defence stayed strong but Nevin got through with a juddering right towards the end and edged the round by a single point. Campbell had a 9-8 lead going into the most important three minutes of his life.

Remarkably, given the stakes, Campbell produced one of his best rounds of the whole tournament with a mature, disciplined and ruthless display of boxing. He would say later that he felt as if the whole two-week experience had aged him three years but he showed no signs of fatigue as he set about 23-year-old Nevin. Midway through the round, with the fight still delicately poised, Campbell caught Nevin with a jab that, combined with a loss of balance, saw the Irishman fall to the canvas. As Nevin looked up at the cameras above his head before springing to his feet in an act of defiance, the crowd that had been chanting

"Campbell, Campbell" throughout the fight roared their approval.

Whether or not Nevin thought it was a slip was irrelevant as the referee gave him a standing eight count. Such a decisive blow in a professional fight might have signalled the beginning of the end but in an amateur contest it counted only as one point for the Hull fighter. Sensibly he did not go looking for the kill, a decision that took an incredible amount of will power. Instead he stuck to his game plan of counter punching, and although he got caught by a couple of right hooks, they were matched by further shots from his powerful left that shook Nevin's head guard.

The bell tolled at the end of a heart-stopping final round, and the two fighters immediately embraced. As they parted, Campbell raised his hands to the crowd sensing he had done enough to win. The cracks of emotion had already begun to appear on the face of the Hull fighter moments later as the ring announcer declared Luke Campbell to be the Olympic champion and the tears began to flow for the boxer who had given so much of his life chasing the title he craved.

Before setting off on a lap of honour around the ring - when he saluted every corner of the arena - Campbell went to Nevin to raise the vanquished fighter's glove one last time.

"'Can't believe it, I've won', that's what was going through my mind," he said of the moment his 14-11 victory was announced. "It's what I've dreamed of for a long, long time and for it to actually be here and to have achieved my goal... I'm lost for words. I didn't want to think too much about the gold as I progressed through the tournament. I had a job to do. I knew I had a lot of hard work to go through.

"This gold means everything. My family, my city - they've all been so supportive of me. A lot of my family and friends have seen how much discipline and commitment I've put into the sport. They're so proud of me and I'm happy that I've made them proud."

Luke Campbell's golden glory was yet another example of true Yorkshire grit by one of the county's Olympians. Raised in humble surroundings by the family of a coal miner, with a brother serving in the forces he sees as the true hero, Campbell had shown what can be achieved with dedication, desire and honest endeavour. Forever striving to improve himself, he had overcome an indifferent start to life in the ring, Beijing disappointment and a trying period when he considered hanging up the gloves, to reign supreme on the greatest stage of all.

The final flurry of the young man from Hull was the last gold won by an athlete from Yorkshire, and the last of 12 medals garnered by White Rose competitors. But for pure emotion and inspiration, it was one of the best.

8. LIZZIE ARMITSTEAD

Only in Britain could the most glorious period of sport unfold against the backdrop of the wettest summer in decades. The afternoon of Sunday, July 29, on the first weekend of London 2012, was no exception. What began as bright morning sunshine soon gave way to torrential rain and there was an unseasonal chill in the air on The Mall as noon approached.

Either side of the famous boulevard, people lined the narrow chute upon which the Olympic women's cycling road race would start and finish, determined not to be swept from their prized seats by the threatened deluge. The anticipation among the crowds in prime position along the finishing straight and out across south-west London and northern Surrey was palpable, as was an increased level of anxiety. Medal competition was a little more than 24 hours old, but the host nation had yet to register a podium finish.

The previous day, Mark Cavendish had been unable to deliver what many had forecast would be the first title of Britain's summer gold rush. Predicting comfortable victories, no matter who the favourite, is a foolish pastime, particularly in an event with as many intangibles as a cycling road race. Yes, Britain had the reigning world champion in Cavendish and the man who had won the Tour de France six days earlier, Bradley Wiggins, backing him up. But there were another 139 riders representing 62 nations who believed there was no foregone conclusion, and so it proved as one by one the British men, tasked with controlling the pace to enable Cavendish fresher legs for the sprint finish, struggled to sustain the tempo. By the time a breakaway had pulled clear in the latter stages of the 250km race, Cavendish's hopes were long gone and the British public's focus on who would be the first hero of the summer had shifted elsewhere.

The women's team of Lizzie Armitstead, Emma Pooley, Lucy Martin and the gold medallist from Beijing, Nicole Cooke, watched Cavendish's race with interest. When their turn came, they would do things differently. There was no overwhelming favourite from the home quartet, and although Armitstead was a strong sprint finisher, this was her Olympic debut.

It was only eight years earlier that the then 15-year-old had decided to take up cycling seriously, after she was identified by a British Cycling talent identification programme. Armitstead had been active in sport all her young life. She won the Otley junior triathlon before secondary school and while at Prince Henry's Grammar, she played on the school's netball and hockey teams, and represented local club Otliensians in hockey. During the summer she competed in athletics.

She was in a Year 11 maths class in 2004 when the cycling talent scout visited the school. "British Cycling had lots of boys signed up from the school, but no girls," explained Sarah Grant, Prince Henry's head of PE and the coach of Armitstead's netball team. "So I just said get the netball team out of class, let's see if there's anyone interested.

"Lizzie already had a natural affinity for endurance sports, with her parents John and Carol, both keen runners. Lizzie did the sprint and endurance tests the scouts conducted, and when she saw her results compared against others from around the country, it gave her the belief."

Armitstead would later acknowledge that moment as the turning point and the wheels had very much been set in motion on a rise that was fast, and not without its controversy.

The speed came in her natural cadence and will to win. Armitstead took to international cycling at a rapid rate, winning a silver medal in the scratch race at the junior track world championships in Vienna, in 2005.

More junior and age-group accolades followed, putting the 19-year-old in the frame for the Beijing Olympics. Missing out on selection served merely to inspire her further and the significant senior honours began to arrive. Armitstead won a host of World Cup races that winter and in 2009 claimed medals of all three colours at the track world championships in Poland, including a gold with the team pursuit squad. Mixing track with road events, she demonstrated equal ability in both and could have gone for gold on either surface at London.

But Armitstead is very much her own woman. While the British track programme provides a support structure offering year-on-year stability for its riders, women's professional road cycling is very much an independent pursuit, reliant on sponsors. Its protagonists require a "have bike will travel" mentality.

That suits Armitstead, who is a free spirit and unafraid to go it alone. In the three years leading up to the Olympics, she raced for teams in Belgium and the Netherlands not knowing at the end of most years where her future lay. To maximise her talents, and fulfil her passion for travel and adventure, Armitstead based herself on the Cote d'Azur, training on the hills in the picturesque south of France; rugged terrain which matches that around her home town in Otley.

And it was on the roads of London where she chose to go for glory at the Olympics, a decision that was fuelled further by the controversial element of her meteoric rise. For the young Yorkshire woman has that all-too-rare quality in professional sportspeople of the modern era, in that she speaks her mind, regardless of the consequences. There was only one incident, coming at the 2011 world road championships in Copenhagen. Yet in an era of instant media it only takes one comment

to transform perceptions and dominate an internet search.

After finishing seventh in the women's road race, Armitstead unleashed a withering attack on Cooke. Armitstead had been the designated leader of the British team but she crashed on the last lap. Instead of guiding the stricken Armitstead back into contention, Cooke took the decision to go for broke herself.

Armitstead accused Cooke of "riding for herself". The accusation would dominate the build-up to the road race. For 10 months, Armitstead and Cooke were confronted with questions about their relationship in every interview they conducted. Was the feud still simmering? Could they race together? Would one sacrifice their ambitions to help the other to the top of the podium?

To her credit, Armitstead handled the regular and uncomfortable inquisitions in a dignified manner, bristling only when the interview focussed too much on the personalities rather than the sport. When I got the chance to speak to her about it on her return to her former primary school, The Whartons, in Otley, in January of Olympic year, she made no apology for what she said in Copenhagen, and even felt that it was right to air her concerns in public.

What it served to do was keep the road race in the headlines, when in any other year it would have been drowned out by the noises the members of the highly successful men's team were making. Armitstead versus Cooke was just as intriguing a subplot as any international rivalries the men's road race could conjure up.

Even as the day dawned, there was no clear leader. Coach Chris Newton had decreed that Armitstead could go for gold if it was a sprint finish with Cooke told she could be aggressive and attack if she felt it necessary. As it turned out on that dramatic day of teeming rain and wheel-to-wheel racing, the 23-year-old from West Yorkshire provided such a courageous and dominant ride that it rendered the question over the validity of Cooke's claims for team leader irrelevant.

If there remained uncertainty about the storm clouds looming over the team dynamic by the time the race started, there was no question what the weather had in store, with the black clouds that darkened the scene below already beginning to empty. The 66 riders edged towards the start line, among them the pre-race favourite Marianne Vos, the 2006 world road race champion from the Netherlands, and Armitstead, who having honed her technique and strength on the wind and rain-lashed roads of Yorkshire, was pleased to see a slick surface and uncomfortable cycling conditions.

The race began just moments after a heavy downpour, leaving the spectators who lined the starting straight to crane their necks above the dripping umbrellas for even the slightest view as the bunch sped past. Contested over a 140.3km course the race was littered with incidents and attacks which delighted the hundreds of thousands that lined the route. Negotiating a clear, error-free path in those early stages was the aim for Armitstead and her team-mates.

The first notable attack on what would be an energy-sapping day was attempted by Ellen van Dijk of the Netherlands after 35km, but she was quickly consumed by the peloton. Van Dijk made a second attempt to splinter the bunch before another of her team-mates, Loes Gunnewijk, attacked, no doubt under instructions from the Dutch team to keep the pace high for Vos later in the race.

Once they had been caught by the peloton, the first significant move by a British rider was made by Emma Pooley, the 2010 world time trial champion. She clung to the wheel of American Kristin Armstrong on the first of two ascents of Surrey's Box Hill, straining every sinew of her body as she kept pace on the 2.5km climb. Box Hill is by no means the Col du Tourmalet in France, but its five per cent gradient and variety of tight switchbacks kept riders who hoped to maintain a fast tempo, out of their saddle.

And so the thrust and parry of attacks and counter-attacks continued, with Pooley and the American trading blows with the Dutch team.

Having allowed Pooley to sap the strength of the bunch, Armitstead first showed her intention to keep pace with the leaders when Vos attacked on the second and final climb of Box Hill.

Armitstead, sensing an opportunity to test the resolve of her rivals, quickly followed, taking Belarus rider Alena Amialiusik with her. Before long, that break too was reeled in by the hungry peloton. But crucially, the continuous attacks executed on terrain made treacherous by what was often torrential rain had taken its toll and those at the front sensed that the next audacious bid for freedom would prove decisive and would leave the chasing pack floundering.

Russia's Olga Zabelinskaya was the orchestrator, attacking on the second descent of Box Hill, around 40 kilometres from the finish line. Pooley went with her to keep her honest, Armitstead having given her team-mate the instruction to go. Pooley's job done, she waved Armitstead on as the Yorkshire woman, along with Vos and American Shelley Olds, joined Zabelinskaya in making an early run for glory.

Those first 20 kilometres of the breakaway would prove the most telling as the peloton, led primarily by the Italian and German teams, attempted to reel in the escapees who had set a relentless pace. Four became three at the front when Olds suffered the heartbreaking misfortune of a puncture.

The peloton kept the time gap below one minute in a defiant bid to not be left behind, forcing the front trio to ride on the rivet. Armitstead, her face specked with mud and soaked by a combination of sweat and the driving rain, took her turn at pacemaking duties with Vos as Zabelinskaya began to tire.

Sensing that the longevity of this breakaway would determine whether she claimed a medal or finished somewhere towards the back of the pack if the race finished in a bunch sprint, Armitstead urged her two rivals to maintain the brutal, lung-busting pace. There was a fascinating dynamic between the three

protagonists, who were opponents from separate countries that would be sprinting for the line against each other in a few kilometres' time. In order to ensure they would have that honour, though, they needed to work together to maintain their advantage, each taking their turn at the front as the other two drafted in behind.

Their persistence was rewarded. The pressure from the peloton eventually eased when a collision occurred on the tight, right-hand corner at the Star and Garter pub in Putney, where 24 hours earlier Switzerland's Fabian Cancellara had seen his hopes of a medal in the men's road race come crashing down.

The three at the front of the women's race were now free to challenge each other for the medals. As they raced past Buckingham Palace and on to The Mall, the lashing rain showing no signs of slowing their pace, Armitstead – with the first British medal all but assured - moved into position to strike for gold. With 300 metres to go she was on the wheel of Vos in second place, who in turn was hugging the back wheel of Zabelinskaya. The Russian had no energy for a sprint and when Vos and Armitstead peeled off with 180 metres to go it was between the two of them for the title.

Vos had the lead and no desire to surrender it as the spray from her back wheel spat up and peppered Armitstead while the headlights of the support car behind illuminated the way to the finish line through the afternoon gloom. Armitstead made a brief lunge down the right, the blindside of Vos, but the Dutchwoman closed the door. Armitstead then moved to the left in one last effort for gold as the two women showed no signs that the last three-and-a-half hours had deprived them of anything left to give.

The crowd in the temporary stands that flanked the finish line rose to their feet, simultaneously applauding the first home medal of the Games and cheering the British favourite on to gold. At road level, on the spectator side of the waist-high hoardings, those fortunate enough to have the best view in the house, banged the sodden boards with the palms of their hands to roar the riders home as Vos and Armitstead powered to the line.

But home support was no antidote to the brilliant Vos's immense power. She stretched her advantage to one bike length, two bike lengths, and refused to let it slip as Armitstead's dream coronation evaporated with every frantic revolution of the pedals.

The Dutch rider, an Olympic champion in the scratch race in the Beijing velodrome, who had broken her collarbone only two months before London, clinched gold in a time of three hours 35 minutes and 29 seconds.

Armitstead, her head crouched over the handlebars as she attempted in vain to rein in her opponent, finished second to win the silver medal. It was mission courageously accomplished. Zabalenskiya, her bronze medal under no threat from the peloton, eased over the line two seconds later.

As the delighted trio slowed to a halt, their legs and arms screaming their discomfort, the race amongst the assembled media to get an immediate response from the newly-crowned Olympic champion and Britain's first medallist began. For those athletes on whom expectation has been misplaced, negotiating a path through the mixed zone can be excruciating as microphones and dictaphones are thrust under noses with scant regard for anything other than a soundbite.

For champions and medallists it offers the first chance to articulate raw emotions that have been pent up for years and are ready to come gushing out like water from a tap. Armitstead, a silver medal hers in all but possession with the ceremony still half an hour and a hot shower away, cut an exhausted but delighted figure.

"It's not gold, but I'm so happy, it's the best day of my life. I'm in shock," said Armitstead, her voice quivering with emotion. "It was so amazing. That final run in with the crowd was

just so special. I've just worked so hard in training and I've had the right people around me telling me I could do it. I'm just so grateful to my family and friends, they're all here and I just felt good. I feel totally shocked, I just want to grab my family and give them a hug...and my team-mates.

"I was feeling a little sorry for them (family and friends in the stands) coming into the run-in, I was thinking they are going to be absolutely scared stiff - so I'm happy."

Credit must go to Cooke, who applauded her team-mate's success, and without whose work Armitstead might not have been able to make the break when she did. Pooley and Martin rightly took their turn to tell their story of the race and heap praise on Armitstead. Vos was also quick to acknowledge the role of the young Yorkshire woman in pushing her to the line with her inexorable determination.

"I knew Lizzie was really fast on the line so I was not at all confident," said the 25-year-old champion. "I knew I had a big chance but I also knew that if I made a little mistake then Lizzie would take the gold."

Away from the mixed zone, observing another triumph for British Cycling from behind the media scrum was Dave Brailsford, the national performance director. Brailsford was the mastermind behind the rise to success of the British squad from the Athens Games onwards, with the exploits of the Olympic team in Beijing and the breakthrough successes of Team Sky's road team, particularly in the Tour de France, owing much to his astute stewardship.

Placing emphasis on sport science, coaching and nutrition at their base in Manchester, Brailsford and his team transformed British cyclists into winners, and thrust a sport that was merely a pastime into one of the most talked-about and well-participated in the country.

Given that it was British Cycling's talent development programme that had discovered Armitstead back in 2004, Brailsford could have trumpeted Armitstead's silver, coming against

65 other riders, as a triumph for the system. But when he was pressed for his thoughts by a group of reporters, Brailsford was in no doubt who the credit should go to.

"It's easy in these situations to look at British Cycling and try and give that some credit, but that result was 100 per cent down to Lizzie," he said. "Lizzie showed tremendous initiative and that was a silver medal won, not a gold medal lost. It was a fantastic performance.

"When you're in a race like that you need guts to go with the break and then commit to it because once you commit you're not going to win if the breakaway comes back to the peloton. You could potentially lose if you don't carry it through, so to commit to that early doors tells you what Lizzie is all about.

"She's got courage, she's very fearless and she's got her reward. Take nothing away from her, she's worked hard, she's been willing to go and live abroad, she's done a lot on her own and she's had to use her own initiative. She decided to commit to the road with the Olympics in mind and what a good decision that was.

"You don't win a silver medal without being able to handle pressure. I think for Lizzie that will be a breakthrough performance."

The rain had become nothing more than a distant memory, a footnote on a thrilling race by the time Armitstead joined Vos and Zabalenskiya for the medal ceremony back under the start-finish line. A refreshed Armitstead strode confidently on to the runners-up podium when her name was called, much to the delight of those who had remained. She waved to the crowd with a broad smile before turning to watch the British flag raised.

Dutch fans, resplendent in their bright orange, had stayed to cheer Vos on to the top step of the podium. But they were outnumbered significantly by home supporters, who applauded with relief and delight. Among them was a strong contingent from Otley, including members of the silver medallist's family.

Lizzie's mother Carol revealed her pride at her daughter's success when she said: "It is more than we could have hoped for."

Grandfather Ray Dunn was torn between emotions at his granddaughter's success. "I was disappointed and delighted," he admitted. "I knew she wanted the gold."

Lizzie's grandmother, Marjorie Dunn, was as enthusiastic a cheerleader as anyone. She stood on the sidelines in the pouring rain in a T-shirt with "I'm Lizzie's Grandma" emblazoned across the front. "A granddaughter who is an Olympian is something very, very special," she beamed.

Later that afternoon, when The Mall had cleared of spectators and the bikes had been loaded on to team vehicles, Armitstead emerged for her press conference. Her medal hanging proudly around her neck and the ceremonial flowers still in hand, she began to expand on the immediate thoughts she had given just 90 minutes earlier.

"It's a strange feeling," she said. "It was just like a dream. It's something you've worked towards for years and it's over in a flash. Winning this medal in front of my family and friends is the most special thing I've ever experienced in my life. It's so crazy and so inspiring."

Of staying true to her instincts and sticking with the break that was made 40km from home, she added: "I'm so glad I committed to it. I was umming and ahhing but I'm really happy I went with it. Our plan was to be reactive rather than proactive. I had to make the call to Emma Pooley whether to attack or not.

"We wanted a select group at the end. We discussed things beforehand about the fast roads coming into the finish and we thought that once you get a committed break up front it makes it hard at the back. I just went with it and I'm so happy it came off. I should have jumped earlier in the sprint, but never mind. Marianne's fast and I'm chuffed with silver."

Indeed she should be. Armitstead's

accomplishment was a triumph for dedication and courage. She could have let the race come to her and taken her chances in a sprint finish, but with customary grit she seized her opportunity and bested all but one of her 65 rivals.

Britain's first medallist awoke the next morning to newspaper headlines lauding her achievement. "Elizabeth the Second" she was dubbed by *The Times*. The picture of her crossing the line in the pouring rain, a half smile creeping on to her face as she simultaneously greeted defeat to a rival and the silver medal, was on the front and back pages of newspapers across the land.

When Britain finally hit the gold trail, with Yorkshire athletes very much to the fore, the unique nature of Armitstead's accomplishment would fade in the public's memory. The fact that she was the first British medallist mattered little to Armitstead, who locked herself away in the opening days, even eschewing the opening ceremony, to focus instead on the road race.

Her Olympics were not done with that thrilling silver. Armitstead was back in action three days later when she finished a creditable tenth in the time trial at Hampton Court, in an event that is by no means her favoured discipline, but one that further illustrated her versatility.

On her return to Yorkshire she was feted at two homecoming pageants, first in Millennium Square in Leeds, and then with an open-top bus tour through Otley when, fittingly, the rain poured.

"I was surprised how many turned up but Otley was packed out," said Armitstead, whose grandmother Marjorie was one of 200 cyclists who followed the bus.

The significance of earning Britain's first medal may not have mattered to Armitstead, but there can be no doubt her magnificent accomplishment set the wheels in motion on an inspirational Olympics.

9. NICOLA WILSON

It was all set. June 14, 2012, would be a special day for Nicola Wilson, the day when all her hard work would be acknowledged, all her dreams realised. After winning medals in every major competition as part of the Great Britain eventing team since 2009, including gold at the European championships in France that year, and another title at the World Equestrian Games in the United States 12 months later, she had established herself as a mainstay of the team.

There was an air of quiet confidence about the 35-year-old from Northallerton, who had first ridden a pony at the age of four. Equestrianism was in her family, and if she received the phone call to say she would be part of the five-person eventing team for the forthcoming Olympic Games that morning it would represent a career high and the culmination of a long, hard, yet enriching journey to London.

Four years earlier she had been the reserve rider for the British eventing team for Beijing. She had been riding *Opposition Buzz* for five years having produced him from a novice, and selection as part of the team was a big pat on the back from the sport's powers that be, and further confirmation that Wilson's career was on an upward trajectory.

That trajectory, she hoped, would reach its peak at London. Although there was an inner confidence about her as she awaited the call that morning, it did not border on arrogance. She knew very well the strengths of the people she was up against for a place in the team. They were good friends, team-mates and confidantes, but at this very moment, they were rivals.

William Fox-Pitt was a team eventing silver medallist at the Athens Games and had won world gold alongside Wilson, as well as individual silver, that week in 2010. Mary King was a veteran of five Olympics and had two medals to her name. Georgina 'Piggy' French was an individual European silver medallist while Tina Cook won team and individual bronze medals in Beijing.

The final name in the melting pot was Zara Phillips, who like Wilson, was hoping to earn selection for her first Games. Phillips was the Queen's granddaughter and the only daughter of Anne, Princess Royal, who in 1976 became the first member of the Royal Family to compete at an Olympic Games, in the equestrian events in Montreal. Zara's father, Captain Mark Phillips, had won gold in the team event in 1972. But she was not just in the equation because of royalty, she could also ride, as she had proven by winning the eventing world title in Germany in 2006. She had been chosen to go to Beijing but had to withdraw because of injury to her horse *Toytown*.

All six riders knew each other well, had competed together and trusted each other. There is a bond between equestrian riders. They acknowledge the work that goes into preparing a horse for competing at the highest level, and they appreciate the danger element that comes with that. It produces a camaraderie among its protagonists. So Wilson was understandably happy that her friends got the call they were hoping for on that morning of June 14.

That she did not, however, left her distraught.

For the second Olympics in a row, Wilson would be the reserve rider. Beijing had been a watershed moment for her, an acknowledgment of her progress that gave her a taste for the Olympic experience. Having been in quarantine with the team and their horses, she was left behind as the team flew out to the Far East. She was heartened to have come so far yet equally determined that she would make the cut for the Games four years later.

To receive the call that she hadn't was a shattering blow for the North Yorkshire woman. "To find I was first reserve was devastating," she said. "It was a real low." But Wilson could not allow her disappointment to be obvious. She had people to stand tall for; her parents, her husband, her staff at their Northallerton yard, and the owner and breeder of Opposition Buzz, Rosemary Search, without whose help and support there would have been no Olympic dream in the first place.

As well as being strong for the people she knew, Wilson also had to field media requests for her reaction. Zara Phillips's selection had piqued national interest. Wilson was considered a surprise omission, given her form during the Olympic cycle and the fact that Opposition Buzz was one of the finest cross-country horses in the world.

Wilson, though, remained dignified and put on a brave face. There was no animosity. Two weeks passed with the heartache festering inside her. Throughout that time, the British eventing team kept her spirits high and refused to let her get too downcast. Performance manager Yogi Breisner was in regular contact, encouraging her to keep herself and Opposition Buzz focused and healthy.

Wilson was deeply moved by the interest the team retained in her. She knew injury or illness could befall any one of the five riders or their horses, such was the sport, but she had resigned herself to the fact that she would not be competing at London. Wilson went to the Barbury International Horse Trials in Wiltshire at the end of the month and showed no effects of the disappointment with a consummate ride. It was a gutsy performance from the Yorkshire woman whose professionalism was impeccable. Putting on such a brave front, though, had taken its toll and the emotions of the past two weeks came flooding out of her

as she opened up about her disappointment to Rosemary Search.

Piggy French was also at Barbury. Riding DHI Topper W, she finished third in the CIC two-star class. It was a ride that pointed to a combination in good form going into the Games. But on July 2, just 26 days before the start of the Olympic eventing competition, fate intervened. French's horse Topper was found to have suffered an injury that ruled the pair out of London. Nicola Wilson, having spent the past three weeks disconsolate that the greatest show on earth would be passing her by, was suddenly thrust back into the spotlight. She would be going to the Olympics after all.

The natural reaction to such good news would commonly be one of unbridled elation, yet the overwhelming emotion for Wilson was of sympathy for her good friend French. "I felt so gutted and disappointed for Piggy because I would never wish that on anybody," she said. "I was surprised at how gutted I felt. It took a while to put that behind me. I was shocked and amazed at how things had turned out.

"The whole period was an emotional rollercoaster. I had been telling myself that far worse things were happening in the world and I was trying to stay positive. That's the thing with horses, you're riding high one moment and on your bottom the next."

Just as there had been little time to let the disappointment consume her, so there was no opportunity for Wilson to allow this rekindled excitement to dominate her mindset. With so little time to prepare, she had to focus on the task at hand.

Breisner had no fears that she would not be up to speed quickly with the team. And before she knew it, Wilson and the eventing team of Phillips, King, Cook and Fox-Pitt were arriving in London on the Tuesday before the Games to finalise their preparations for an event that would begin just four days later.

The spotlight in the build-up shone brightly on Zara Phillips, with the Queen's granddaughter growing increasingly disappointed at the

constant questions surrounding her family at the pre-event press conference. To the wider world, Phillips was the big news story of the equestrian competition. To Wilson and the rest of the team, she was just Zara, an invaluable member who was not placed on a pedestal by anyone, especially herself.

Phillips's presence gave the sport the publicity it craved, but with that increased exposure came added scrutiny. An example of that came on the morning of the opening ceremony, when every member of the eventing competition has to parade their horse in front of a panel of judges and vets, known as the ground jury. It's a routine drill to check the welfare of the horse. If a rider and their support team have not been looking after their mount in the proper manner they can be expelled from the competition, even at that late hour.

Wilson, having already suffered Olympic disappointment once that summer, was not about to let anything jeopardise her hopes again, and left no stone unturned in preparing *Opposition Buzz* who passed with flying

colours. As did every member of the British team, except Phillips, who was asked by a vet to take her horse High Kingdom on a second run in front of the jury. It created a flicker of controversy among the gathered media and photographers, when in reality it was nothing more than routine, and she eventually passed.

On the bright morning of Saturday, July 28, at Greenwich Park - a picturesque course with the imposing London skyline providing an urban backdrop to the rural setting - the Olympic eventing competition began.

The event – which is akin to a triathlon as it tests the all-round ability of horse and rider - was split into two medal competitions. The five-person teams would do battle over three disciplines and four days for the collective title, with the individual element running concurrently. Team and individual competitions used the same scores, with two days of dressage, followed by the cross-country on Monday, and the show jumping on Tuesday. The three lowest scores of the five riders would count towards the final tally.

Just four weeks after thinking her Olympic dream had been ruined, Wilson rode Opposition Buzz into position to begin Great Britain's bid for team glory in the dressage. She was desperate to do well, particularly in the team event. What she was not expecting, though, was a crowd as big as the one that greeted her at Greenwich. Wilson had competed in some of the biggest events in the world but nothing could have prepared her for the wall of noise she was greeted with from 50,000 spectators.

"When I got out there the crowd erupted," she said. "The number of people was staggering. It took your breath away. I was very emotional, and it made you proud to be British." The reception was something she would never forget, but if she didn't focus and deliver her best performance that memory would have been tinged with regret.

The definition of dressage is "the highest expression of horse training" where "horse and rider are expected to perform from memory a series of pre-determined movements". Dressage is a test of the controlled but undetectable relationship between horse and rider, developed over hundreds of hours of training. The key is to portray harmony and free-flowing movement, giving the impression to the judges that the horse is doing all the work on its own. Judges award and deduct points for each series of manoeuvres, with the total score then converted into an overall percentage, which in turn is converted into penalty points.

For Wilson, it was also a test of keeping her emotions in check. The excitable reception and constant support had to be blanked out, because it could harm a dressage performance. If she was tense and nervous, then that would be transmitted to Opposition Buzz, and mistakes would follow. Wilson maintained her composure the entire time and her score of 51.70, although not as strong as Mary King's 40.90, was enough to put Britain into silver-medal position overnight.

"I was delighted with the dressage, he stayed with me, he was a true professional," said Wilson. "I was so proud of him. Over the years we had built up a level of implicit trust."

The following day, amid a thunder storm, Phillips, Fox-Pitt and Cook took their turns at dressage with Cook's score of 42.0 and Fox-Pitt's 44.10 putting Britain into third place of the 13 teams after the first stage. Wilson was 39th overall out of 65 riders, but the cross-country the next day was when she would excel.

Where Opposition Buzz had shown his dexterity in the dressage, on the cross-country course where rider and horse had to negotiate 28 obstacles, he would show strength and courage. Again Wilson would be first out for GB. She had plotted the course five times, measuring it out for time intervals and then setting minute-markers on her stopwatch that would indicate to her during the run whether she was inside or outside the required time. The purpose of walking the course was also an attempt to predict where problems might

occur. The task was to complete the course without running out or stopping at a fence, which would result in time penalties, or falling off, which would mean elimination. All of that had to be done inside 10 minutes and three seconds.

As first out, Wilson's job was to go clear within the time and then report back to her team-mates about difficult spots, places to attack etc. She felt under enormous pressure as she made her way to the start line. Her nerves were so high she had to struggle to contain them, but at least that adrenalin kept her alive to the dangers that lay ahead.

Again the crowd cranked up the noise levels. "It was like galloping into a tunnel of screaming," said Wilson. As the stopwatch on her wrist – in sync with the scoreboards around Greenwich Park - ticked down from 10 seconds to zero to signal the start of her run she could barely hear it. As the ride unfolded, with rider and horse so far executing a flawless run, Wilson began to panic. Through all her years of competing her stopwatch had never failed her, yet on the biggest stage of all, she had not heard it beep to signal the first minute-marker she had so carefully plotted out earlier that day. It forced her to take her eyes off what was in front of her and look down at her watch to check it was working, because without it she was progressing on feel alone. Her watch, though, was working perfectly. The beeps had merely been drowned out by the unabated noise of the crowd. And Wilson was bang on her minute-markers.

That knowledge filled her with confidence and, remaining focused the entire way round, she completed the course inside the time and without incurring a penalty. It was a terrific ride. As she returned to the stables she was mobbed by her team-mates who had been inspired by her run. She then reported back about the nuances of the course before taking her place alongside her team-mates to support each of them as they took their ride. Even then, Wilson found she was just as nervous watching as she had been riding.

As she watched, the work behind the scenes that ensures all riders have their horses in the best of conditions for the final day began. Lynn Swift, who had been Wilson's head groom for 10 seasons, ensured *Opposition Buzz* cooled down as quickly as possible and got his heart-rate back to normal before taking him back to the stables for a well-earned rest.

Britain ended the third day in second place, behind Germany and in front of Sweden, New Zealand and Japan. That night the team headed back to the athlete's village, Wilson and the other women in one flat, Fox-Pitt, Breisner and the support team in the other. Over dinner they discussed tactics for the following day and tried to keep thoughts of medals at bay.

Wilson, having excelled in her favoured cross-country, went out second in the show jumping under leaden morning skies. Wilson could hear a pin drop as she prepared to begin, an eerie quiet that was just as daunting as the deafening roar of the preceding three days.

A horse's energy and obedience are under the microscope in the jumping, which was conducted over 12 jumps across a 500-metre course. It also tests the mental resolve of the rider, as Wilson found after she knocked down the second fence on her round. Instead of letting that worry her, Wilson put it to the back of her mind instantly and concentrated on finishing the course without any more mistakes.

That one error resulted in four penalty points which meant a total of 55.70 and kept Britain in the hunt for a gold medal. Fox-Pitt had earlier executed a flawless run. Both he and Wilson had actually done enough to progress to the final stage of the individual round and compete for medals – for which the top 25 do one more show jumping round. But because Britain already had three competitors in the top bracket, they had taken up their quota of challengers. It was galling for Wilson, but her mind stayed switched on to following her team-mates' progress.

Over the next two hours the team competition

ebbed and flowed. Phillips went next, and like Wilson clipped an early fence. She also incurred a time penalty that dented Britain's hopes for the gold medal. They still lay second, with Germany now almost secure in gold-medal position. The Swedish and New Zealand teams were breathing down their necks.

Mary King had a nervy moment over the Stonehenge Combination of fences but she rode clear on *Imperial Commander*. The German team, coached by Yorkshireman Chris Bartle, who ran the Yorkshire Riding Centre near Harrogate, secured gold with their penultimate run. As Tina Cook began Britain's final run, she did so with the hosts holding a slender 0.2-point advantage over the third-placed Kiwis. Cook needed to be flawless, and with the crowd on the edge of their seats, Cook and mount *Miners Frolic* went clear with a breathtaking run to clinch the team silver to the delight of a jubilant crowd.

It had been an anxious few hours, fitting really, considering the emotions Wilson had lived through over the past seven weeks. But it was all worth it as she celebrated a silver medal on her Olympic debut. Her score might not have been taken into account in the final tally as the lowest three scores are used, but even if it had

been it would still have been good enough for silver. On all three days she had done her job to the best of her ability and her flawless ride in the cross-country, in particular, had set the tone.

"We were delighted to come away with something," she said. "We all wanted to win. It's what you train for all those hard winter mornings in the rain, the snow and the cold. But to come away with silver was an amazing achievement. My overwhelming emotion was relief that I had put in the best performance I could."

Aptly, the Princess Royal – who had watched on alongside the Duke and Duchess of Cambridge and Prince Harry – presented her daughter Zara and the team with their medals. The royal approval provided another of those iconic images of an Olympics laced with emotion.

"I was proud, honoured, relieved and a little emotional standing on that podium," said Wilson, who barely a month earlier had resigned herself to her Olympic dream being crushed. But all that was now forgotten as the Yorkshire woman who had been riding since she was four stood proudly on the podium, her lifetime's ambition fulfilled.

10. TOM RANSLEY

Tom Ransley and the other members of the men's eight rowing crew did not go to London 2012 merely to compete and enjoy themselves. They did not become Olympians to parade around in their Team GB uniforms, getting pats of encouragement on the back and gratitude from the regular man in the street. Not even the rare chance to bump into Usain Bolt in the food hall at the athletes' village served as motivation.

They qualified for their home Games, fought their own individual battles to take a seat in such a prestigious boat, for one reason only - to win gold. The chance to become an Olympic champion, to write a small chapter in the rich history of the biggest sporting event on the planet, does not come along very often. And the purpose of the crew at Eton Dorney in the first week of the Games was to fulfil a lifetime's ambition and crown a four-year cycle of the hardest work they will ever undergo by claiming the ultimate prize in sport.

So when they only took bronze in the final it felt like a dagger to the heart. To most athletes, an Olympic bronze is celebrated as a victory and something to cherish for the rest of their days. For the admirable members of the British rowing squad, to whom winning is everything and losing is nothing, it felt like defeat. Even worse, failure. The collective disappointment with which they greeted third place, their faces etched with despair as the exhaustion eased and the hurt sunk in, illustrated the winning mentality of British rowers.

To outsiders, those on the banks who cheered when they saw on the scoreboard that Britain had hung on for third, and those watching at home who had moved to the edge of their armchairs, fists clenched as they willed the home crew to give one last final push, the octet's heartache rammed home just how much the Olympics meant. In their sheer desolation, they gained empathy from the watching millions. Too often in this country, participation means more than winning. In the highly successful rowing squad, the mantra "go hard or go home" applies. If you're not in it to win it, then don't bother turning up.

The manner in which they had achieved third place, having gone all out for victory by bravely dictating the tempo to a German crew that had not been beaten since 2009, endeared them to the watching public.

In the immediate aftermath of defeat, such empathy did not register with the British men's eight of Constantine Louloudis, Alex Partridge, James Foad, Richard Egington, Mohamed Sbihi, Greg Searle, Matthew Langridge, Ransley and their cox, Phelan Hill. In time, the wounds would heal, and when they looked back in the weeks and months that followed, they could reflect on Olympic bronze as indeed an accomplishment. Even though they felt like throwing their medals into the serene waters of Eton Dorney after collecting them on that sunny day just 60 minutes after their defeat, one thing was clear, the three crews who filled places fourth to sixth – United States, Netherlands and Australia – would gladly have swapped with them.

Just to reach that dramatic, brutal final, 26-year-old Ransley had not taken the orthodox route into rowing. A big, powerful man by the time of the London 2012 Games, standing 1.98m tall and weighing 100kg, his passion for rowing was only reignited eight years earlier when he attended York University.

Born in Ashford, Kent, on September 5, 1985, Ransley rowed as a teenager for his local club. But when he moved up to York for university in the summer of 2004, he feared he may have

to pack his oars away for good. What he found in the historic city was a very progressive rowing club on the River Ouse.

Ransley cut his teeth at York City Rowing Club, a proud organisation boasting 200 members that had been prominent in the city since the 1840s. Ransley was taken under the wing of some of their veterans and his desire for the sport was given cause to burn brightly.

"If it hadn't have been for York City Rowing Club I would have probably had to quit rowing," he said in October, 2011. "I was looking for a club that matched the intensity of training I knew down south, and they were the ones. I really felt like York and Yorkshire embraced me."

And Ransley embraced the social scene as much as the rowing aspect of life in North Yorkshire. He was made to feel welcome by the university and the rowing club. He spent three years rowing for the club, winning the Henley Regatta with them in 2007, and even when he left the University of York to continue his education at Cambridge before taking up the sport full-time upon his graduation, he continued to name York City Rowing Club as his affiliation. He still did as London 2012 approached, such was the affinity with the club, its people and the city.

Ransley began to make in-roads into the British rowing scene while in York and by the time of his switch to Cambridge, in 2007, he was representing his country in the men's eight. They finished fifth at the European Championships in Poland, and sixth in the world Under-23s championships in Scotland.

Ransley's first international medal came in the week of his 23rd birthday in Serbia in 2008. He won a bronze at the university world championships as part of a developmental coxless four, made up of Ransley and three other Cambridge oarsmen he had rowed with in the University Boat Race earlier that year. But it was as part of the men's eight that he began the long road to London. He won a pair of silver medals in World Cup meets in 2009 in the eight, and finished fifth in the world championships that year in Poland.

It was not until 2010 that the men's eight established themselves as genuine challengers to a German crew that was now beginning to dominate. Britain's silver medal at the world championships of 2010 in New Zealand, was a significant step up for the crew. They finished only six tenths of a second behind the Germans. Twelve months later the gap might have extended a little, but they again won world silver in Slovenia, behind a German octet that was under no illusions as to the size of the challenge they would face in a year's time at the Olympic regatta.

Despite the high standard, Ransley and his team-mates greeted a second successive silver as defeat, a sign of the huge expectation they were fearlessly burdening themselves with. As they headed into Olympic year, with the pressure on individuals to earn a seat in a competitive boat just as intense as the collective challenges they were facing, Ransley underlined his importance in the No 6 seat, in the engine room of the boat, with a series of sterling performances.

In March he partnered Greg Searle to sixth place in the men's pair at the British trials. The appearance of Searle was helping thrust the British men's eight into the spotlight and keep their exploits in the headlines. Searle was the 40-year-old veteran who won gold with his brother Jonny in the coxed pair in Barcelona in 1992, and a bronze four years later in Atlanta in the coxless four. He had retired once, but had come back to bolster the men's eight for one last shot at Olympic glory. Searle had been in the men's eight that picked up silver medals in successive world championship finals prior to the Olympics. As well as those two, Matthew Langridge, Alex Partridge and Richard Egington were all driven on in the lead up to London by the disappointment of Beijing, when they were part of the crew that won silver.

With the make-up of the men's eight still to be decided, Ransley and company finished second in Belgrade, three tenths of a second behind the Germans in the opening World Cup regatta at the beginning of May. Later that month in Lucerne the British eight gave the German crew an almighty scare when they pushed the favourites all the way to the line, eventually succumbing by the narrowest of margins.

The men's eight arrived in Munich in mid-June for the final regatta as favourites, with both world champions Germany and Olympic champions Canada absent. Illness in the crew prevented the Germans from competing, but Britain only managed third behind Poland and Australia.

Despite the disappointment, the men's eight was still a competitive boat and at the beginning of June, Ransley's selection to compete in his first Olympics was confirmed and the crew headed to a high-altitude training camp in Austria. Ransley went into his first Games with a simple motivation. "For me it's the recognition that this is the pinnacle of what I want to achieve in life and that is enough for me," he said.

The chance to fulfil that ambition began on the morning of Saturday, July 28. Memories of an awe-inspiring opening ceremony at the Olympic Park the previous evening were still fresh in the mind as the first fans poured through the turnstiles and security checks at picture perfect Eton Dorney. With the sun shining brightly, there was no mistaking the feel of the first day of an Olympics - the tension

among the crews was evident, while the excitement at the prospect of the next two hours of racing and two weeks of sporting drama rippled through the temporary stands that flanked the Buckinghamshire water.

The host nation's first test would ultimately set the tone for how they would approach their greatest challenge, because lining up alongside them in the second of two heats was the German boat. The Canadians were also in the heat, along with the Netherlands, leaving the crews of each boat under no illusions as to the size of the task, even at this early stage. Only the first boat across the line would qualify automatically for Wednesday's final, with the next three forced to go through Monday's repechage.

The British crew were bolstered by the return of their powerful, 20-year-old stroke Constantine Louloudis, who had missed much of the build-up due to a back injury. Old Etonian, Louloudis – who has a Greek father and a mother who is sometime lady-in-waiting to Anne, Princess Royal - had been rowing on his school's water since it was opened in 2006. But Louloudis and the crew came out of the blocks slowly and, after a sluggish 500 metres, had to dig deep to row through the Canadian and Dutch eights. The Germans, though, only reinforced their status as favourites with a dominant performance. They crossed the line first in five minutes 25.52 seconds to qualify for the final, with Britain coming home in five minutes 27.61 seconds.

With a 48-hour turnaround before the repechage, there was little time to brood over

that opening defeat for Ransley and the British eight. They had to find early speed from somewhere, and a tactical breakthrough was also the order of the day. With four of the six boats progressing to Wednesday's final, Monday's repechage was as much about rediscovering a coherent rhythm and laying down a marker as it was winning outright.

Encouragingly, they managed all three, making them believe that an extra race might have been a good thing after all. Sensing they needed to start quickly, the GB eight did so, and roared on by a crowd of 25,000 up near the finish line, they led reigning champions Canada at every 500-metre marker as they kept their tempo and stroke-rate high.

They crossed the line in five minutes 26.85 seconds, having made light work of a nuisance cross-wind. The 'Deutsche Achte' may not have been quaking in their boots as they observed from the banks, but they were certainly aware of the threat from the home boat as the day of the final dawned.

Yorkshire Day actually proved to be a breakthrough for British Olympians, as after the first four days in which no gold medals were won, home competitors finally started to deliver to the relief of an expectant nation. Later that day Bradley Wiggins would add time trial gold to the historic Tour de France victory he had claimed only a week-and-a-half earlier, while on the water at Eton Dorney, Britain's first gold was won by the incomparable, inspirational duo of Heather Stanning and Helen Glover in the women's pair.

Just 20 minutes after that, with the emotions

still raw and a current of excitement and anticipation coursing through the stands, the six boats that would contest the final of the men's eight were manoeuvred to the start line. This was it for Ransley, Searle, Louloudis, Partridge, Sbihi, Egington, Langridge, Foad and cox Hill. All the hours of burning muscles, bursting lungs and screaming limbs had come down to this. Their moment of truth had arrived. If they had any chance of beating their German rivals, the general consensus was that they would have to dictate the tempo by taking the fight to the favourites.

Ransley and the boat's leaders knew this all too well. What it led to was a breathless final, one of those sporting occasions that gets the heart pounding against the rib cage, not only for the protagonists but for those on the sidelines, willing them on. The British eight, from lane two, with the German crew two lanes to their right in four, exploded out of the blocks like a shot from a cannon. With Hill barking instructions and encouragement from the cox seat, every Briton in that boat, from Louloudis in the stroke seat to Partridge in the bow, via Ransley in the engine room, strained every fibre of their being to maintain a coherent, powerful stroke rate.

The energy of the crowd, still buzzing from witnessing that landmark first gold just minutes earlier, inspired the British crew who held the lead at 500 metres. Buoyed by the start they had made, they kicked on and kept their inexorable rate high. By halfway, the possibility of a gold medal against the best crew in the world was growing ever more real with every slash of the water by the harmonious oars.

The British were flying, but they had reached an early crescendo, and there was still a little more than a quarter of the race to go. To their left as they looked across the water, the green boat of the German crew, which had been fully visible in their eye line for the best part of 1,500 metres, began to disappear from view as their leadership of the race ebbed away. Two thousand metres over six minutes is a hell of a long way, particularly in such a high stakes race when emotions and mental reactions have to be managed as acutely as physical strain. The British crew were running on fumes over the closing quarter. They had nothing left to give. Only the desire to finish what they had started, to cross the line giving everything they had, drove them on.

As the German crew surged through them towards their rightful destiny, continuing their relentless, phenomenal stroke-rate, they took the Canadian crew in lane five with them. Canada had not been a feature for 1,700 metres of the race but sport is how you finish, not how you start.

Britain, cheered to the line by screaming fans whose involvement in the race had been heightened by the home boat's bravery, dug deep into their energy reserves to stay the course. The German crew of Filip Adamski, Andreas Kuffner, Eric Johannesen, Maximilian Reinelt, Richard Schmidt, Lukas Muller, Florian Mennigen, Kristof Wilke and their cox Martin Sauer had too much for them. They crossed the line first in five minutes 48.75 seconds.

Canada took second, while Ransley and the British crew, under pressure from a late-surging United States, Netherlands and even Australian boats, hung on for third. Britain's time was five minutes 51.18 seconds. The U.S. were only three tenths slower, the Dutch and Australians all within three quarters of a second. Had the race gone on another 100 metres, Britain could have finished last. Conversely had it been over 1,400 metres, they would have been Olympic champions.

But the final was over 2,000 metres. As the Germans celebrated as their boat drifted almost apologetically towards the pontoon, the British crew slumped over each other in exhaustion and despair, their hands dropping over the side of the boat into the chill water.

As the crowd greeted ecstatically the news that they had clung on to third place and won the bronze medal, there were no such thoughts of celebration in the minds of Ransley, Partridge, Searle et al. What was a victory for courage was in reality, a defeat. They had gone all out for the gold medal and the honour of being

Olympic champions in front of an adoring home crowd, and nothing else mattered.

"We came here to win," said Ransley, in a statement that was echoed by each member of the crew with whom he had shared, invested and sacrificed so much. "I never thought I would say I'm not happy with an Olympic medal, but I'm not. We gave it our best shot and went for broke, that's why we're in third, not second.

"We were keeping ahead of the field and thought we were moving through and it was in the last 500 metres that it started to fall apart because we were trying to get our bow in front. We gave it our all. A bronze medal is no consolation. We wanted to be in the final so we would have an opportunity to win gold. A few years ago I wouldn't have dreamed of this. We row so well as a team and we expect to win. That's what we train to do. We've been the second best boat all through the season and bronze isn't a true reflection of where we are. It's no consolation."

Their faces at the medal ceremony later that morning only reinforced those emotions. Even the most distraught of Olympians who consider bronze a failure can usually gather the pride to muster a smile when they are presented with their runners-up medals.

There was not a smile to be seen on the faces of the British crew. Ransley looked like he had just been told his house had burned down such was the solemn look he wore. There was only cause for a wave to the crowd in acknowledgment of their unequivocal support.

As the days wore on, however, and the memorable London 2012 narrative unfolded, the magnitude of the accomplishment of being an Olympic medallist began to sink in for Ransley. By the time he returned to York in the middle of August, a little over two weeks after the final, he did so with the bronze medal hung around his neck.

There was a modicum of pride as he sat by the River Ouse – remembering the hard hours spent on the water with York City team-mates he considers close friends – and the reality dawned of just how fortunate he is to have an Olympic medal to his name.

"It's definitely good to come away with a medal," he reflected. "Especially when you consider all the injuries that you could get, or even a cold that you could get on the morning of the race that could undermine you. We still have no regrets about the way we went after the gold. That was our best way of winning the race, even if it cost us the silver. I am really glad people can see that, because that's certainly the way we approached it."

11. PARALYMPIC HEROES

Seventeen days after the Olympic Games finished, the Paralympics began amid an equivalent amount of fanfare and excitement. London and the people of Great Britain did not treat the event for disabled athletes as the poor relation of the Olympics it had been made to feel like in the past.

From its inception as an event for injured war heroes at Stoke Mandeville Hospital in Buckinghamshire in 1948, through its first official staging in Rome in 1960 and beyond, the Paralympic Games had been little more than a mere afterthought for host cities that placed considerably larger stock in hosting the Olympics. Even as recent as the Atlanta Games of 1996, Paralympic athletes competed in empty stadiums as buildings in the athletes' village and the Olympic Park were being destroyed around them.

Sydney four years later was the breakthrough Paralympics, when disabled athletes finally began to be embraced as equals. There was a gradual increase of interest through Athens and Beijing when organisers realised that if Sydney had raised the bar they could not be the country guilty of taking the highest-profile sporting movement back into the dark ages of inequality.

London went one better. It was a breakthrough Games for the Paralympics, an event staged on the same scale as the Olympics, with as many volunteers, as much colour and as much hype. Over the preceding 12 years the Paralympics had grown into the second largest sporting event on the planet, purely because of the numbers of people taking part. At London those vast numbers of participants, nearly 4,300, were dwarfed by the hundreds of thousands of spectators who attended the event.

Stadiums and arenas that were full just weeks before, were packed to capacity once again as the watching nation became hooked on wheelchair basketball and seven-a-side football. Athletics and swimming again took pride of place in the showpiece venues around London's Olympic Park as the 12 days of the Paralympics from Wednesday, August 29, to Sunday, September 9, again lived up to the Games motto to 'inspire a generation'.

It was an awe-inspiring event, where disabled people demonstrated what can be achieved no matter what the perceived limitations. The Paralympic movement already had its superstars. South African Oscar Pistorius, the 'Blade Runner', had competed in the Olympics just a few weeks earlier, reaching the semi-final of the 400m before competing with his compatriots in the final of the 4x400-metre relay.

South African swimmer Natalie Du Toit was a household name in sporting circles. Britain, too, had its heroes whose deeds in disability sport transcended boundaries. Dame Tanni Grey-Thompson was the face of the British Paralympic movement for 16 years. From Seoul in 1988 - which set the trend as the first host Olympic city to also stage the Paralympics – to Athens, the wheelchair sprinter from Cardiff won 16 medals, 11 of them gold. After her retirement, Britain gained a new darling in 13-year-old swimmer Eleanor Simmonds of Walsall. Simmonds – who has achondroplasia, a common cause of dwarfism - captured the imagination of the nation in Beijing, winning two gold medals in swimming's S6 category, despite being the youngest member of the British squad.

In London, more heroes emerged as the host nation's disabled athletes built on the monumental success of their able-bodied counterparts by winning 120 medals, 34 of them gold. And just as Yorkshire's Olympians had figured prominently earlier in the summer, so too did the county's Paralympians, with two in particular to the fore.

Halifax's wheelchair sprinter Hannah Cockroft and archer Danielle Brown from Lothersdale, near Skipton, cemented their burgeoning reputations with gold-medal performances. Cockroft was one of the myriad feel-good stories of the Paralympics. At 20, she was the smiling face of the British track team. As ebullient a character as you are likely to meet, she lit up the Olympic Stadium with two dominant performances in the T34 100m and 200m sprints.

Like all disabled athletes, her journey to the top of the medal podium was one to tug on the heartstrings of even the most hardened of individuals. Cockroft suffered two cardiac arrests at birth that damaged two parts of her brain. The resulting damage left her with deformed legs and feet and weak hips, as well as problems with balance and motor skills. Her parents were told Hannah would be unlikely to live past her teenage years.

Cockroft, though, is the kind of person who does not like to refer to her disability, classified as cerebral palsy, as a hindrance. She can walk a little, albeit almost bent double, but she has a heart as big as anyone. She had a passion for sport in her youth and at the age of 13 her father, a welder, built her a racing chair.

In 2007, after winning a silver medal in the seated discus in the UK School Games, Cockroft was invited to Loughborough for a British talent day where she was encouraged by Ian Thompson, husband of Tanni Grey-Thompson, to try an elite racing chair. Cockroft fell in love instantly.

By the end of 2008 she had been invited into the British Paralympic squad and within two years Cockroft - in a chair she christened 'Sally', donated to her by a local dance academy - was eating up world records at a terrific pace. She made a statement of intent on the global stage when she won two gold

medals in the T34 100m and 200m at the world championships in New Zealand in January, 2011.

Then in May, 2012, on the track where Usain Bolt, Jessica Ennis and Mo Farah would set pulses racing later that summer, Cockroft claimed the distinct honour of being the first person to break a world record in London's Olympic Stadium. She stopped the clock at 18.56 seconds in the 100m.

Her star was rising so rapidly that she was already one of the poster girls of the Paralympics, along with the likes of Simmonds, long before the second instalment of the inspirational Olympic summer began. The British public knew they had a star on their hands, and the way they greeted her into the stadium for her first heat in the T34 100m on the morning of Friday, August 31, sent shivers charging down spines just as rapidly as they had done four weeks earlier when Ennis took her first steps into the Olympic cauldron.

Cockroft admitted afterwards that the "mind-blowing" noise the sell-out crowd had generated for that morning session had "scared" her. Yet, just like Ennis, Cockroft used that energy to fuel her speed. If there was any fear she did not show it as she obliterated the competition in her heat, to the extent that she could freewheel home over the final 25 metres. Even then, that was quick enough for a new Paralympic record of 18.24 seconds. She had already lowered the world mark to 17.60 seconds at a meeting in Switzerland, shortly after the test event in London.

On her return to the track that evening, Cockroft – whose earrings were the Yorkshire White Rose - was again visibly moved by the cacophony of noise that cascaded down the banks of the Olympic stadium. They were there to hail a new hero and in rip-roaring fashion this human drag racer did not disappoint.

Hunched forward on her chair in lane seven of the final, Cockroft looked like a bullet in a loaded gun. When the pistol went off she set off down the straight as if the back of her chair was turbo charged. Her arms pumping in

controlled fury, Cockroft had the lead after only 10 metres and there was only going to be one outcome. She crossed the line with nothing around her but the copper-coloured track. It was not so much a race as a procession, leaving the question of who took silver and bronze redundant as the gold-medal winning performance was marvelled at.

Cockroft's face, one that is so often warm with delight, contorted into momentary disbelief, as if after all she had been through in her life this was just too much to comprehend. But any negatives soon evaporated as she began her lap of honour in a stadium she had sent rocking. Cockroft soaked up the acclaim of a crowd that had been moved to tears by her courage, her bravery and her sheer speed. The Olympic Stadium was hers.

"I kind of was deciding whether to cry or laugh or what to do," reflected Cockroft on her emotions as she crossed the line in a new

Paralympic record of 18.06 seconds, which was staggeringly, one-and-a-half seconds quicker than silver medallist Amy Siemons of the Netherlands.

"It's a little bit surreal when you've been dreaming about it for so long and then it just kind of happens in, what, 18 seconds? You're kind of like, 'I want to do it again. I can do it better.' But I've got it now. I can't complain. As the gun went off it just erupted in here and it was amazing. I loved it."

Six days later, 'Hurricane Hannah' as she calls herself on the social networking site Twitter, blew through the Olympic Stadium again. This time it was the T34 200m, her strongest event, as if her rivals needed further cause for trepidation. In the call room before the final, one of her opponents went up to Cockroft and in an attempt at gamesmanship, said: "Just take it easy on us today, Hannah." Quick as a flash, and offering no ray of hope to her rivals,

Cockroft responded: "I'm not here to be nice to you."

The only people she had smiling a few minutes later were the 80,000 people in the stadium on what was another night of majesty and emotion. Jonnie Peacock shocked Oscar Pistorius and the world when he won the T44 100m title while David 'the Weirwolf' Weir won his third of four gold medals in the T54 800m. And Cockroft again displayed her brilliance to win the 200m title just as comfortably as she had claimed gold in the 100m.

Again she was in a league of her own, setting off from lane six and overtaking the two women on her outside within 20 metres, such was her raw pace and power. As she came into the home straight, the crowd rising to will her on to even faster speeds and extraordinary feats, Cockroft remained focused on the finish line.

As she crossed in a Paralympic record time of 31.90 seconds, having reached a top speed of 17mph, Cockroft punched the air and screamed with delight as the stadium erupted in unbridled joy. Just as the Olympic experience emboldened Leeds boxer Nicola Adams with a sense of belonging, so the Olympic Stadium instilled in Cockroft a genuine belief that she was born for the spotlight and to compete on the biggest stage.

On another golden night for British sport, Cockroft had sealed her status as one of the most emblematic figures of the London Paralympics. And she could have had more accolades had the 400m and 800m events – which she was world record holder in – been classified as Paralympic disciplines.

As it was, the two gold medals she won raised controversy among her peers who believed that because she had the ability to walk – although with great difficulty – she was wrongly classified. But Cockroft refused to let the controversy cloud what had been a phenomenal accomplishment, or the truth that there was no-one to touch her.

"I used to get a lot of comments saying I was

a cheat and a fake," said Cockroft. "But I have all the doctors' notes proving I am in the right class. There are so many athletes winning by massive amounts here. It is either they're training harder or they've overcome their disability in a different way. There's no real answer to it. I'm not really bothered by the comments any more. Whatever – I've got two gold medals."

Indeed she had. Halifax's Hurricane Hannah had written another inspirational chapter of the Olympic summer.

While Cockroft was wowing the crowds in the Olympic Stadium, Danielle Brown was confirming her reputation as one of the finest archers in the world, regardless of disability. The 24-year-old from Lothersdale near Skipton went into London as Britain's equivalent to South African sprinter Pistorius.

In Beijing, she had won gold in the women's individual compound, which was accomplishment enough for any Paralympian. Yet Brown sought to demonstrate her eye for the target was as good as anyone's, irrelevant of disability, at the Commonwealth Games in Delhi in 2010.

The Leicester University law graduate suffers from reflex sympathetic dystrophy in her feet, which means she has to compete either sitting down or leaning on a stool. But she was just as deadly with her compound bow, as she and team-mates Nicky Hunt and Nichola Simpson beat Canada in the team compound final to win the Commonwealth title. She also reached the quarter-finals of the individual event. But it was her gold in the team event that completed a unique double for the 22-year-old Yorkshire woman who had bridged the gap between disabled and able-bodied athletes.

Going for an unprecedented double by combing the two at London 2012, however, was unrealistic as the compound bow was not allowed in Olympic competition, only the recurve bow, which Brown did not enjoy using. With her sights fixed firmly on gold in the individual compound at the Paralympic Games, Brown had none of the distractions

that the increased publicity of a double bid across two Games would have brought.

Instead, her campaign began in the relative calm of the Royal Artillery Barracks in the ranking round on Thursday, August 30. She demonstrated her strength in the competition when finishing top of 12 competitors in the ranking round, and then expressed disappointment at her score of 676 from 72 arrows, because it was 21 down on the world record score she set en route to the European title two years earlier in France.

What worried her was that it was her lowest ranking-round score of the year. What heartened her was she had two days to go away and work on her technique. If she was hoping her nerves would have eased by the time of the quarter-final against Maria Rubio Larrion of Spain, she was mistaken. Brown was still not in top form as she took a 2-0 advantage in the first set. After the second was tied, she allowed her opponent to level before eventually securing a 6-4 victory in the fifth and final set.

Brown's nerves at least reminded her of how much a successful defence of the title meant to her, and it also ensured she was not too over-confident to allow complacency to creep in. She was more like the world's best she had become since winning the first of three world titles in 2007 when she defeated Marina Lyzhnikova of Russia 6-2 in the semi-final on Tuesday, September 4, to set up an all-British gold-medal shootout with Mel Clarke just 30 minutes later.

In a tense final at the Royal Artillery Barracks, the Britons could not be separated, drawing 27-27 in the first set and 29-29 in the second, before three arrows into the nine saw Brown, who was shooting first, take a 4-2 lead. Clarke responded to take the fourth set 29-26 and level at 4-4 to force a fifth. But Brown dominated the final set and 30-year-old Clarke, who required a maximum 10 score on the final arrow to tie, shot a seven - her worst arrow of the final - as the pressure told.

Brown had won and her emotion at defending

her title at London 2012 was more relief than anything else. "I've really been feeling the pressure the last couple of weeks," she said. "So to actually come here and manage to keep my head in the right place, I'm chuffed to bits about that. It's been crazy. I didn't think it would have affected me the way it has."

Another Yorkshire-based Paralympian striving to defend his titles at London was 31-year-old David Stone, who suffers from cerebral palsy. Stone, originally from Birmingham, had been a member of the British ParaCycling team from 1995 to 2000, and attended the Sydney Paralympics in his final year before quitting the sport.

On his return at the end of 2004 he enjoyed far greater success. In Beijing he won the gold medals in both the CP1/3 time trial and road race. Ahead of London he was fearful that the gap had closed since Beijing and his concerns were proved prescient when he lost his gold medal in the mixed T1-2 time trial at Brands

Hatch, taking bronze. But the cyclist who trains with able-bodied riders around his home in West Yorkshire, bounced back with customary defiance to win the T1-2 road race in front of a jubilant crowd at Brands Hatch.

Claire Cashmore was born in Birmingham without a left forearm but that never prevented her from being a fine swimmer. She was up at 5.15 every morning to train at the John Charles Aquatics Centre in Leeds – her base since moving to the city to study in 2006 - proving it was not only able-bodied athletes who put their all into their golden quest.

Cashmore won three bronze medals across two Paralympics in Athens and Beijing, and in London arrived determined to go two better in at least one of the events she raced in at the atmospheric Aquatics Centre. In two of those races in London, Cashmore went one better, winning silver in the SB8 100m breaststroke and another silver in the 4x100m medley.

"It was amazing to be on the podium seeing all my friends and family in the crowd, I just wish it was us with that gold medal around our necks," said Cashmore, who swam the breaststroke leg of a race in which they were beaten by Australia by three one hundredths of a second. Cashmore also added the bronze 4x100m freestyle relay.

Halifax-born Karen Darke left London with one medal and a place in the nation's hearts for one of the more touching moments of even that emotional summer. The 41-year-old, who was paralysed from the chest down at the age of 21 after a sea cliff climbing accident, won a silver medal in the women's H1-2 cycling time trial. But it was what she did with team-mate Rachel Morris in the women's H1-3 road race that so endeared her to the public. The two Britons had matched each other spoke for spoke on their hand cycles and crossed the line together holding hands, just as the Brownlee brothers had done in their pre-Olympic triathlon in Oxfordshire in June. They wanted to share the moment, although the photo finish declared Morris to be the first across the line for bronze.

"We worked so hard together over the last few years," said Darke, who had in the past hand-cycled the length of Japan. "We couldn't bear the thought of pipping each other to the line. It wasn't that one of us was stronger than the other so we just thought 'let's do it, let's grab our hands at 50 metres and go'."

The life of Dewsbury's Robin Womack was turned upside down when he suffered a prolapsed disc in 2003, but he got into athletics while in rehabilitation at the spinal unit at Stoke Mandeville Hospital. He won a bronze medal in the men's F54/F55/F56 shot put after throwing a personal best of 11.34 metres.

James Crisp, 29, who was born in Nottingham but had represented City of Sheffield swimming club since he had moved to Yorkshire to attend university, had been a Paralympic phenomenon in 2000 and 2004, winning 11 medals, three of them gold. Having missed out on Beijing because of a shoulder injury he added to his tally in London with a silver in the S9 100m backstroke.

The British table tennis squad based at Sheffield's English Institute of Sport won a record four medals. Will Bayley, 24, won silver in the class 7 men's individual, and bronze in the men's class 6-8 team event with Ross Wilson and Aaron McKibbin. Sara Head won a bronze with Jane Campbell in the C1-3 team event.

There was many a story of triumph over adversity from the Paralympians of Yorkshire, Britain and the wider world during 12 days of exhilarating action. The entire Olympic summer showcased sport at its finest and Britons at their most generous and gracious.

Time and again the spirit of the nation was raised by the deeds of the country's athletes, and throughout the entire summer Yorkshire's inspirational, dedicated and talented athletes ensured their achievements would linger long in the memories of the millions of people fortunate enough to witness such wonderful sporting drama.